The Hunger Diseases

Raymond Battegay has written an important book. He has taken his years of rich clinical experience and combined them with his knowledge of physiology and shared with the reader a larger picture of hunger and its meaning. His ability to capture the panorama is of immense value to the practicing clinician and those health professionals who have a specific point of view. What the author has done is to stimulate the reader to think about the larger meaning of hunger and its relationship to narcissism.

Like a fine composer, the author has established the main theme and has developed the symphony. This book belongs in the library of every clinician as well as student of human behavior. The book is more than a "how to" manual; rather, it concerns itself with "how to develop your own approach" to major clinical problems. The clinical practicioner will find specific answers. More importantly, he or she will find a theoretical framework so that a therapeutic intervention may be attempted.

Max Rosenbaum, M.D., Palm Beach, Florida

This is not just another book dealing with conflicts between psychoanalytical concepts or theories. On the contrary, it is a work where the author uses his experience to describe, as he points out in his preface, the common traits of individuals who refuse food, and those who overeat.

Bernardo Blay-Neto, M.D., São Paulo, Brazil

The author skillfully places psychiatry back within medicine by systematically studying how hunger integrates mind and body in a wide clinical spectrum. He also presents hunger as being at the core of the culture of narcissism, which is characteristic of this century, thus broadening the understanding of our contemporary society.

Ramon Ganzarain, M.D., Associate Professor of Psychiatry,
Emory University, Atlanta, Georgia

The Hunger Diseases

Prof. Raymond Battegay, M. D.

Foreword by Prof. Otto F. Kernberg, M. D., New York

Hogrefe & Huber Publishers
Toronto • Lewiston, NY • Bern • Göttingen • Stuttgart

Library of Congress Cataloging-in-Publication Data

Battegay, Raymond
[Hungerkrankheiten. English]
The hunger diseases/by Raymond Battegay; foreword by Otto F.
Kernberg
p. cm.
Translation of: Die Hungerkrankheiten
Includes bibliographical references and indexes.

1. Eating disorders. 2. Self. 3. Narcissism.
4. Starvation—Psychological aspects. I. Title.
[DNLM: 1. Eating Disorders—psychology.
2. Psychophysiologic Disorders—etiology. 3. Starvation— psychology. WM 175 B335h]
RC552.E18B3813 1991
616.85'26—dc20
DNLM/DLC
for Library of Congress90–1563
CIP

Canadian Cataloguing in Publication Data

Battegay, Raymond
The hunger diseases

Translation of: Die Hungerkrankheiten.
Includes bibliographical references and index.
ISBN 0-88937-054-0

1. Eating disorders. 2. Compulsive behavior.
3. Hunger–Psychological aspects. I. Title.

RC552.E18B313 1991   616.85'26   C91-09350-3

© Copyright 1991 by Hogrefe & Huber Publishers

12–14 Bruce Park Ave.	P.O. Box 51
Toronto, Ontario M4P2S3	Lewiston, NY 14092
CANADA	USA

Printed in USA

ISBN 0-88937-054-0
Hogrefe & Huber Publishers, Toronto • Lewiston, NY • Bern • Göttingen • Stuttgart
ISBN 3-456-81990-0
Hogrefe & Huber Publishers, Bern • Stuttgart • Toronto • Lewiston, NY

❖Table of Contents

❖Foreword

Contemporary psychoanalytic theories of early development converge in their focus on the importance of the originally dyadic nature of human experience. In other words, the building up of an internal world that reflects the intersubjectivity of the infant-caregiver relationship is considered the basis for both normal and pathological formation of psychic structures. The experience of being loved is intimately connected with the capacity to love oneself and to love others. The failure to develop a harmonious infant-caregiver relationship may derive from the infant's inborn abnormalities in the development of affective structures, in metabolic responses to early feeding and physical care, a constitutional hyperactivity or incapacity to respond, but is for the most part owing to the infant's failure to experience "good enough" mothering. Such failure in early caregiving may lead to pathology in psychic structure formation, affecting self-esteem regulation and self-love as well as the capacity for loving others. All these conditions are encapsulated in the syndrome of pathological narcissism.

Following his investigation of the psychological and biological consequences of pathological narcissism in an impressive series of contributions over many years, Professor Battegay brings together in this volume the concept of an abnormal "hunger for love" in a vast array of psychological and psychosomatic pathology. He suggests that, after initial failure in the gratification of both narcissistic needs and object relations, an excessive hunger for love deteriorates into a self-defeating, insatible need for narcissistic gratification, which constitutes the common thread of apparently disparate types of pathology. From the concretization of psychological hunger in the disturbances of physiological hunger in the eating disorders to the vicissitudes of the narcissistic personality disorder; from the narcissistic conflicts in severe depression to the psychological complications of diabetes; from the hyperactivity and aggressiveness of "type A" personality structure in patients prone to cardiovascular illness to the relentless search for power and sadistic control in patients with malignant narcissism, Professor Battegay traces a common thread of insatiable psychological hunger.

Under pathological circumstances, what originally was the basic need for acceptance, love, and reciprocity in human relations miscarries into the destructive forces of greed and voracity, envy and devaluation, regressive fusion, and the dismantling of what is incorporatied. These dynamics evolve as overwhelming unconscious dynamics that underlie the clinical syndromes mentioned and others which are related. Professor Battegay illustrates how these developments can lead to suicide and criminality, and how biological predisposition and psychological developments interact.

Professor Battegay draws on a broad spectrum of psychoanalytic theories and findings, and brings together the formulations of alternative psychoanalytic approaches to normal and pathological narcissism. Perhaps in providing a comprehensive view of the field, he does not do full justice to the incompatibilities between some of these theories, and by concentrating on psychodynamics rather than on the psychological structures that result from these dynamics, the internal contradictions within the field are left unexplored. By the same token, however, this very insistence on psychic motivation over the different structures of the many types of psychopathology brought together in this volume manages to produce a comprehensive view of the many ramifications of narcissistic conflict.

Vivid clinical illustrations convey the dramatic nature of narcissistic pathology as a major problem not only in psychiatry but in medicine in general and in the social field as well. While Professor Battegay's focus is on phenomenology and psychodynamics more than on psychological treatment, his case material reflects both the help that psychoanalytic psychotherapy may provide as well as the limitations of therapeutic interventions with patients who have already managed to significantly destroy their life options, and where psychopathology and sociocultural limitations conspire to seal a patient's destiny.

Professor Battegay's direct, comfortable, and easy style, and his avoiding, wherever possible, technical language should make this book accessible to the educated layman as well as to the specialist in the field. It is a welcome contribution to what might be considered a very European approach to bridging biology and psychology in a unitary vision of illness that incorporates the biological, psychodynamic, and sociocultural determinants of psychopathology.

Associate Chairman and Medical Director, The New York Hospital-Cornell Medical Center, Westchester Division;
Professor of Psychiatry, Cornell University Medical College

Otto F. Kernberg, M.D

❖Preface to the German Edition

Since the beginning of my psychiatric activities in 1953, I have come to recognize how much certain patients depend on the doctor's encouragement. Depressives of all kinds, but also individuals who are dependent on drugs, prescribed medicines or alcohol, appeared to me to "hunger" more for emotional warmth and stimulation than other people. Over the years it became clear to me, partially also through my reading of the corresponding literature, that "hunger" represents not only an oral need, but also a wish and desire for narcissistic fusion, for a reinforcement of the self in individuals who, in their early childhood, did not receive enough warmth or who were excessively cared for and subsequently resented an emotional emptiness—but as well in people who, in their early childhood, had to live according to parental ideals and were not able to develop a consistent self. These individuals suffer from a narcissistic neurosis (narcissistic personality disorder in the sense of Kohut [1971/1977]) with a deficiency in their self-esteem (Battegay, 1977/1979).

It is certainly not by chance that in a time in which people are growing up in small families, in which social cohesion is diminishing despite increasing support through social networks, many people do not feel that they are being recognized, confirmed or understood enough as individuals and thus suffer from feelings of loneliness.

To many patients I owe my gratitude for the knowledge that arose in the course of my medical activity. Also the many discussions with my colleagues have enlarged my view. Special thanks are due the late Dr. Martin Bandmann, Tel Aviv, former Head Physician of the Second Department for Internal Medicine at the Beilinson Hospital in Petah Tikvah, Israel, where I worked as an assistant physician in the years 1954/1955. To Prof. Udo Rauchfleisch, psychologist at the Basel University Psychiatric Outpatient Clinic, I am grateful for the examination of my manuscript and for his criticism and the corresponding valuable stimulation he gave. Equally, I owe gratitude to Professors Willi Berger, M.D., and N. Gyr, M.D., as well as to Dr. Ch. Perini, M.D., from the Basel University Department of Internal Medicine, who examined my manuscript with respect to somatic data. My thanks also to my secretaries, Ursula Häberli and Rosemarie

Dufner-Stump, who have typed the manuscript in an excellent and careful manner. Finally, I wish to thank my wife, my two elder sons and their wives as well as my youngest son, not only for their suggestions, but especially for the patience they had with me in spite of my seemingly endless professional activities. Here, I would also like to thank Mr. Heinz Weder and his co-workers at the publishing house Hans Huber for their cooperation.

Now the book should speak for itself. I am aware that the subject has not been treated comprehensively, but it was my wish to direct a spotlight onto the "hunger diseases."

Basel, June 1982
Raymond Battegay, M.D.

❖Preface to the German Paperback Edition

The enlarged paperback edition of my book speaks for the fact that the problem of inner emptiness, of being unfulfilled, and of uncertainty in the realm of self-esteem is indeed widespread and has in fact become a cultural phenomenon not only in Western, but also in Eastern society. Humans today are overwhelmed by stimuli, they are chasing even more ardently after new experiences, are afraid of not being recognized in their own character and generally not being acknowledged sufficiently. As hungry persons who are continually aiming to incorporate objects and/or to take possession of them by phantasized fusion, they are constantly experiencing refusals—and thus remain hungry. In this book I have reviewed the different kinds of hunger diseases and showed the different forms of hunger states in their various psychopathological dimensions as well as discussing the therapy thereof. This is not meant as a comprehensive treatment, but rather gives suggestions and impulses for professionals and interested lay people.

Basel, Autumn 1986
Raymond Battegay, M.D.

❖Preface to the English Edition

The term "hunger diseases" is used for all those states in which—because of narcissistic and oral needs—people are driven to consume objects—and/or to take possession of and to consume them—in an addicted manner. As soon as such objects become part of the concerned people, they no longer exist for them, and other objects have to be sought anew. I have tried to describe the common traits in individuals who refuse food and in those who overeat, in people who are depressive or addicted, in diabetics and in patients with gastrointestinal disturbances as well as in those who are driven to perpetual activity until they suffer from cardiovascular disease. In special chapters I discuss the psychological problems of people suffering from emotional hunger during and after long-lasting situations endangering life or suffering from physical hunger. Finally, the insatiable hunger of dictators to take possession of and to "swallow up" as it were continually more countries and thus to increase their power is shown as consistent with the psychodynamics of persons suffering from hunger diseases. Certainly, the hunger phenomenon can be observed in many more aspects of human life, for example, in the expectations of human beings toward each other, but it is the intention of these reflections to remain within certain boundaries.

The author wants to express his gratitude to his secretary, Miss Elisabeth Kurer, for helping him to translate the German text, and to Mr. Joseph A. Smith of Hans Huber Publishers for editing the final English version.

Basel, January 1991
Raymond Battegay, M.D.

❖General Considerations

Never again is it so easy for humans to get food as in the mother's womb. In the milieu of the maternal uterus, the warmth stimulates one's physiological functions and guarantees, at the same time, one's well being. At birth, we are forced to leave the maternal body. The child is pressed out into a cool world—especially in our civilization and at our geographical latitude. Otto Rank (1924) spoke of the birth trauma humans have to undergo. The first manifestation of a newborn baby is therefore a cry, which contains both the narcissistic injury of being expelled from the maternal body as well as the imperative demand for restitution of the homeostasis that reigns in a mother's body. Many facts indicate that children whose mothers had insufficient quietude and leisure to lend them attention while in the womb do not experience this "elated elation" (Grunberger, 1971) that would have prepared them for life after birth; in this new social environment they will suffer from hunger for restitution of the lost (or never experienced) equilibrium: They will therefore cry for it. In this cry is contained also the aggressive demand for that human presence that provides security and allows one to experience warmth and stimulation. The human child, who, as Portmann (1944) correctly states, enters the world too early in comparison with other primates' offspring, is not yet able to get around alone and is totally dependant on the help of the mother or other people. Not even the regulation of one's own body warmth is possible in the first months of life. Children therefore need a "social uterus" to feed them, support them, and give them security and stimulation.

The hunger for tactile closeness, for warm care, and for stimuli characterizes the first months of life of the human child. The skin has the important role of not only setting boundaries to the outside world, but also of serving as a communication organ. Sigmund Freud (1961/1963) overevaluated food intake by stressing orality in the first phase of the child's development. In the end, it is unimportant whether the nourishment offered is of an artificially manufactured or of a natural form, i.e., as breast milk: *The way nourishment is offered is essential.* Even during the feeding of artificial food, the mother's skin contact is of utmost importance. In natural feeding, it is the contact with the mother's breast, certainly also within the realm of orality, that mediates to the baby a convincing closeness, offering the child security and shelter. The child's cry at the moment of birth—which does not exist in every culture, especially not in those in which newborns are laid at once on their mothers' warm skin—signifies accordingly the expression of a hunger that emerges when intrauterine homeostasis is lost and consequently frustration of not being cared for results. Strong babies tend to urge, through phonetic intonation, more intensively than weak ones their mothers' care. The child therefore also determines how much care and tenderness a mother grants her offspring. Besides the mother's primary motivation, also the secondary one—provoked by the baby's demonstration of hunger—counts.

Use of the term hunger in the broader sense thus includes all those manifestations that embrace a human being's active, "aggressive" desire not only for (oral) nourishment with food, but also for emotional, warm (tactile) attention. With this one satisfies the longing for contact and communication, but also for stimulation—something well founded within every human being. This hunger for human nearness characterizes us in such a way that one could easily say: Without other creatures' approving and testifying, a human being would not be a human being. Only this "hunger" for a group of persons equally driven and of similar constitution makes one a human being. When isolated, humans cannot secure their own existence.

With love, "hunger" is intensified to an extreme. The union of two people could not occur without this longing for a loving fellow human being. The mutual attraction of the sexes can thus also be regarded as a "hunger," and hence we speak of love's "hunger." Individuals who have not experienced in their early childhood the warmth and stimulation all humans need for healthy development, will hope—mostly in vain—all their lives of having that powerful and tender experience they are missing. But because of their early deficiency, they will entertain such high expectations toward all persons they meet that they usually remain "hungry " even after a corresponding encounter.

To a certain extent everyone wants to be admired, with the possible exception of those who like to or are all too willing to subordinate themselves to others, a kind of "masochistic triumph." Managers who reach the top of the ladder—and this is especially true for politicians—are often people who show a "hunger" for power. Their greed for power may be so great that they strive to take possession of ever more objects, thereby already sowing the seeds for their later fall from power. Their "hunger" has mislead them into such "devouring" that they necessarily demise as they can no longer digest what they have embodied. Such a "hunger" for power often occurs in persons who did not experience the necessary leisure, calmness and parental attention in their early childhood because of difficult family situations, broken homes from one or both parents missing, or because of growing up with foster parents or in a home (Rentchnik et al., 1977). Later in life such persons need more and more people to satisfy their "hunger"—and yet they are somehow never able to satisfy it. The heads of state of countries ruled authoritatively develop such a "hunger" for power that they are effectively insatiable and continuously threaten to swallow up whatever proves to be weak. The surrounding states or the political partners are often appeased by such persons—like in the fairy tale, where the wolf was able to devour Little Red Riding Hood and her grandmother after having declared his innocence and masked his aggressive hunger.

People who have been neglected in early childhood tend to have narcissistic injuries and often a tendency toward enormous outbursts of rage and vengeance. In some, the "hunger" for revenge increases to an uncontrollable, insatiable and repeated desire to hurt the people around them who—often only in their imaginations—have offended them. These enormous tendencies toward vengefulness may have pushed many persons into National Socialism in Germany in the 1920s, 1930s and 1940s. With the help of fellow party members, they expected to be able to satisfy their "hunger" and to play out their cruel and vengeful feelings. By letting innocent people starve in concentration camps, by torturing, violating or—under frightful conditions—murdering them, they fancied themselves exalted in their compensatory fantasies of grandiosity meant to cover up their feelings of inferiority. The "superman" delusion pushed them to even greater atrocities. Millions of individuals lost their lives to satisfy the cannibalistic "hunger" of the Nazis—and to allow them feel superior to those who were unable to defend themselves against such incredible cruelty.

Within the normal range lies the "hunger" for action or activity. Our nervous system needs constant stimulation in order to preserve its balance. If one is cut off completely from any outside interferences through "sensory deprivation" (Lilly and Shurley quoted in Gellhorn & Loofbourrow, 1963; Gross & Sváb, 1969), it takes only 10 hours until one starts to hallucinate. When unable to perceive anything in the environment, one apparently stimulates oneself. Corresponding changes can be observed in the EEG. The "hunger" for signals, for stimuli, and for Gestalt-cognitions is a normal psychological phenomenon. There thus exists a "hunger" for ever new experiences.

A human being is marked, since birth, with a "hunger for love," which—as mentioned—results in the newborn baby seeking attention through articulation. The "hunger for love" accompanies us throughout life and leads us to be constantly on the lookout for a partnership. If our "hunger" is insatiable, we live in unsteady relationships, always expecting to find the final satisfaction of our desires for nearness and our "hunger for love" elsewhere.

People who have not experienced enough warmth and stimulation in their childhood and have received only insufficient possibilities of Gestalt-cognitions, or who have been supplied with an excess thereof and are therefore secondarily frustrated, end up with a lifelong "hunger" for loving attention that can scarcely ever be satisfied (Kohut, 1971, 1977). Such persons long to experience an object through which they, on the one hand, can be convinced of the readiness for a partnership and, on the other hand, of their own self-value.

René Spitz (1957, 1960) observed in a study with 91 babies in an orphanage that children did not develop properly who were given to the home after having been nourished at their mother's breast for 3 months. The physical care for the children was good, but a female attendant had to look after ten charges or more at the same time, so that they received only one-tenth of the normal maternal emotional attention and were thus emotionally deprived. These children developed month by month an ever more pronounced clinical picture that was proportionally linked to the duration of the separation from their mother. During the first month, the children cried a great deal, were very demanding and hung onto the observer who entered into contact with them. In the second month, their crying changed to screaming; at the same time, weight loss and a standstill in their development occurred. In the third month, the children refused contact, and a pathognomic position was observed: They mostly lay in their beds flat on their stomach. Their sleep was disturbed. They continued to lose weight and frequently suffered from recurring diseases.

Generalization of the motoric retardation and rigid facial expression were registered. After the third month, the facial rigidity remained stable. The screaming was replaced by a soft whimper, the motoric retardation by lethargy. At a follow-up control, 34 of the children observed had died within 2 years. The described process was reversible up to the fifth month if the child were given back to the mother. Spitz (1957/1960) considered this disorder a symptom of "hospitalism." He called the condition "anaclitic depression," referring to the picture of adult depression.

These observations in babies demonstrate how much a child's development depends on the emotional attention and the stimulation it receives. Such extremes of emotional deprivation occur only rarely, but even a minor deficiency can lead to a lifelong defect: An (insatiable) emotional hunger remains, and the individuals concerned are unable to experience real encounters, supportive communication with another person, since they always have the tendency to take total possession of or to incorporate the object into themselves. Result: The object loses its character as a separate entity.

Even a short separation from the mother—lasting only a few days—during the first 2 years of life may have serious consequences if there is no one else present to fill the gap and to respond to the baby's needs (Bowlby, 1973, James and Joyce Robertson, 1975). Even after such short experiences of separation, such children may behave aggressively headstrong for some weeks, refusing food and for years becoming anxious when the mother is not where they expect her to be. This emotional deprivation, experienced over a period of a few days, disturbs their appetite and their sleep, and causes them to be aggressive toward their closest person of reference, the mother, thus showing her, on the one hand, that they still feel "hungry," and, on the other hand, that they want to punish her for the pain they had to endure.

Through experiments with monkeys (Harlow, 1962, 1967) it was possible to show how important it is to the development of living creatures that they experience warmth. The two Harlows let half of the monkeys grow up with a mother surrogate consisting of an iron-wire construction with milk bottles attached to it. The other half of the monkeys grew up with a mother surrogate covered with a synthetic fur (terrycloth) and equally with fixed milk bottles. The small monkeys nourished by the fur substitute mother developed an emotional relationship to their mother surrogate similar to that of young monkeys to their real

9

mothers. When in danger, they sought protection near the "fur mother." The monkeys who knew only the iron-wire mother did not show any emotional relationship with the mother surrogate, nor did they seek protection from it when in danger. The reproduction of the animals growing up with the iron wire construction was also disturbed, while the generative functions of the monkeys growing up with the fur mother remained intact, and the animals increased in number. Later on, the "fur mother" was separated from the small monkeys by glass, and it was observed that the mere sight of the fur mother calmed the young monkeys down when anxious. The visually perceived fur mother produced a positive reaction in the small monkeys even in quiet situations.

From G. Benedetti (1976) I received the personal communication that when the iron-wire construction with the attached milk bottles was moved, the young monkeys growing up with it developed normally. Of course, we cannot transfer all conclusions from animal experiments to human experience. Through Spitz's (1960) trials with a face mask we know that 3-month-olds smile only when the mask is moved. Mothers know intuitively that they have to move their head along the frontoccipital plane if the child is to smile. These experiments also indicate that, besides physical and emotional warmth, the child needs stimulation through movement and through possibilities of Gestalt-cognition (e.g., face or face mask with marked mouth, nose and eyes). If too little of this is offered to the baby, it remains "hungry."

"Hunger" concerns not only the stomach, but also the narcissistic elements in humans. If as a baby an individual does not receive enough affirmation in form of warmth, stimulation and cognitive possibilities, it remains unsatiated in its self—it remains "hungry for love." But also children who receive too much care will suffer from this emotional "hunger" in later life, since no one will be able to replace such early-childhood "spoiling." This "hunger for love" means that the people in question experience throughout life a painful emptiness in their self, in their self-value, and they will do almost anything to put an end to this state. In this context, it is interesting to note the German proverb: "Die Liebe geht durch den Magen" ("The way to a man's heart is through his stomach"). What is meant here—only the nourishment itself or rather the consumption of dishes prepared and offered with love? With the latter, filling the stomach would not be the main criterion, but the "fulfillment" of desires meant to "fill up" the "unsatiated" self. It is not only a question of

10

satisfying our oral needs, but rather one of receiving warm and supporting attention from others, in other words, so-called narcissistic gratifications through objects. In the long run, nobody can exist in emotional coldness.

Life in a concentration camp was perilous not only because of the atrocious and constantly immanent menace of being exterminated, it was also constantly threatening because of the annihilation of the human beings in an atmosphere of perpetual coldness, hostility and cruelty. The people concerned were often marred in their self so much that they identified themselves with the enemy and were seized by a feeling of their own worthlessness. It is known from various authors (von Baeyer, Kisker, 1960, Lempp, 1967, Eitinger, 1969, Eitinger and coworkers, 1985, and others) that former concentration camp inmates were scarred by those events so much that they later suffered from depressions, anxieties, distrust and psychosomatic disorders. In these camps, human existence was tormented and dishonored by starving and with all methods of torture to such an extreme that survivors were later nearly unable to live with the depletion of their self and their cruel and hypertrophied superego. Many of these people may have perished not only because of lack of food, but also because of the total lack of respectful human attention. They remained hungry in every respect, starving not only because of missing food, but also because of the complete absence of any sign of humaneness on the part of their guards.

When we speak of hunger in this way, we mean not only the suffering linked to not being satiated and the desire for physical appeasement, but as well the wish for emotional warmth and fulfillment. As we all know, "man does not live by bread alone," but equally—or even more so—from emotional satisfaction. Certainly, human attention acts (for example) through emotional impulses—which have a somatic substrate in the limbic system— in the human approached in this way. However, it remains hidden to us what exactly "leaps" from one individual to another in such an emotional act. Although somatic processes are known to be evoked by human interaction, the problem of what forms it remains unresolved. Is it, for instance, only the information concerning the benevolent attention an individual receives through the mimic and pantomimic expression as well as through "eye language" and verbal expression? The fact is that whoever is unable to experience an empathic interest from others remains hungry.

As the comments up till now show, the "hunger" phenomenon is based on a very complex psychosomatic process. Since no psychic experience is imaginable without a somatic substrate (and the term "hunger" obviously includes the somatic state), the neurophysiological as well as the metabolic aspects of the problem will have to be discussed in the following. With respect to the "hunger" for love, for attention and for stimulation, from the somatic point of view it is known to date only that the nervous system needs external stimuli in order to remain in balance. As far as the somatic substrate of the "hunger" feeling with respect to food is concerned, the results of several studies are more varied (Brobeck, 1979). We will discuss these matters in the chapters on *Anorexia nervosa* and *Obesity* in more detail.

❖Anorexia nervosa

Hetherington and Ranson (1940) discovered that bilateral lesions in the ventromedial hypothalamic zone of rats led to hyperphagia and obesity. According to Smith (1976), Anand and Brobeck (1951) reported that rats in which a lesion had been made in the region of the lateral hypothalamus (situated opposite the ventromedial part) no longer ate. The aphagia was dramatic, the rats even walking over the food without grasping it. The food refusal was life threatening, and the rats eventually died, if they were not nourished artificially. Anand and Brobeck (1951) assumed that the ventromedial hypothalamic zone inhibits the need for food. They developed a hypothesis on the central nervous control of food-intake behavior based on the supposition of two brain centers, the so-called "dual-center hypothesis." The ventromedial hypothalamic zone would lead to an inhibition of the food intake ("satiety center," Morley, 1980), and the lateral hypothalamic region would lead to an increase of the food intake ("food-intake center," Morley, 1980).

In 1954, Teitelbaum and Stellar observed that rats with a lesion in the lateral hypothalamic region could recover their eating and drinking capacity if they were nourished artificially long enough. Teitelbaum (1954) supposed that the recovery of food control behavior represents a repetition of ontogenetic development. These researches, however, were to be contradicted by others, so that today they are not yet substantiated. Further research (Brobeck, 1979) showed that electrical stimulation of the ventromedial regions of the hypothalamus led to an inhibition of food intake, and electrical stimulation of the lateral hypothalamic region caused an increase in food intake. The fact that stimulation and destruction lead to opposite results seemed convincing. This argumentation, however, was questioned when it became possible to influence not only the food-intake behavior but also other kinds of behavior through lesions and stimulations in the above-mentioned regions (Grossman, 1975). Alterations of food-intake behavior would, as Smith (1976) emphasizes, represent perhaps only one aspect of an altered sensomotoric integration into the brain. But this supposition is not yet well founded. Other hypotheses of food-intake behavior are considered in more detail in the chapter "Obesity."

From the comments on rat trials it can already be seen that refusal of food not only corresponds to complex psychological behavior, but is also founded on a somatic basis in which manifold neuronal and metabolic processes are active (see chapter on "Obesity"). Of course, the results of these animal trials cannot be simply transferred to humans; rather, they are meant to incite our thinking of the possible somatic background to anorexia nervosa. With food refusal in humans there are certainly manifold other influences such as eating behavior and approach toward food in the family, early learning processes with respect to eating, parents' eating patterns, rejection of one's own sex role and thus also of the corresponding distribution of the subcutaneous fat, and last but not least the insufficient self-identity acquired through experiences of emotional deficiency in childhood. In the following, I discuss some aspects of anorexia nervosa—without, however, setting claim to giving an exhaustive overview.

In anorexia nervosa, those concerned, mostly female adolescents, display their emotional "hunger" by starving themselves physically. They reject the (female) adult role, first, because they have never experienced through their mother the loving care they expected and would have needed for a fulfilled life; second, because this way they are able to demonstrate that they have remained "hungry" emotionally. Their malnutrition leads to their scarcely appearing to be females, and they can also openly display their hunger disease in a world of abundance—in a sea of (edible) objects (Sours, 1980). The martyr's picture they present frightens others and motivates them to help. Anorexia nervosa patients apparently gain pleasure, by means of a learning process, in living in this dangerous situation, in this borderline situation between life and death, and they are rarely able to give up their addictive tendency to maintain "thinness." Their desire to do everything to become, on the one hand, omnipotent and independent of food and, on the other hand, to manifest their hunger disease dramatically, becomes irresistable and "insatiable." Often the communication between these individuals and their relatives concerns only eating. The environment tries to blackmail them as to their food intake, and the persons concerned insist more and more upon emaciating their body and idealizing their hunger. Their "thinness" becomes a "monument" to their addictive hunger.

Such was the case with a patient who had been seen repeatedly on a consulting basis in the Basel University Department of Internal Medicine since her 27th year for very severe states of emaciation. Since the age of 13 she had lived in a very grave and extremely emaciated state, and at the age of 17 had to be admitted to a children's hospital weighing only 23.9 kg. She is the daughter of a relatively old father, an academic with a differentiated yet hypersensitive, resentful, hypochondriacal, neurotic personality who takes everything to heart—and who himself has suffered since adolescence from a "nervous" stomach. His resentments toward society were a burden to his family. His wife, who is many years his junior and the mother of this patient, was never accepted by him. He despised her for her alleged poor education, though in fact she is a practical, capable and caring housewife and mother. Yet her word never carried weight within the family. The marriage was disharmonious from the beginning and determined the parent-child relation. The patient's sister, who is several years older than she, aggressively opposed the dominating father. She suffers from a small stature and has had severe emotional crises with outbursts of seething hatred and jealousy toward her younger sister, the patient, whom she experienced as healthy. The patient herself was a timid child who had difficulties standing her ground already in primary school. She was unable to attend high school—as planned by her father—and suffered stomach pains because of the demands of the lower-grade secondary school she finally attended. She experienced herself as a boring and colorless outsider. At the age of 13 she had her first menstruation. At the same time, she started losing weight, and it came to a secondary amenorrhea. She suffered from diarrhea as well as a fear and loathing of vomiting and diarrhea. At the age of 17 she repeatedly threatened to commit suicide. She had a panic fear of meals. A psychotherapy lasting up to the age of 20 had only a short-term success. The doctor in charge of this treatment diagnosed a very early disturbance of the patient's self-representation. At the beginning of the psychotherapy, the patient was convinced of her feeblemindedness and her incapacity to become ever a respectable person. Only a very few well-selected professions were considered honorable in her family. Having been her father's hope and having disappointed him so much tormented and discouraged her. Any demands made of her always led to intestinal symptoms. Her mother was unable to be a model for her, since strictly speaking she despised her mother just like her father did. In the course of the therapy, the patient gained in autonomy, though without developing a consistent self. At age 24 and again at 27 she was hospitalized in a psychiatric inpatient ward, having lost weight down to 27 kg in the first instance and to 23 kg in the second. She showed the same problems known from previous times: the total rejection of herself—as well as of her mother—and the feeling of failure toward her father's expectations. During her last stay in the University Department of Internal Medicine, at the age of 34, she was seized by complete restlessness and walked around the whole hospital with her IVs attached and pulling the support behind her, as if wanting to accuse her surroundings and to show people the awful suffering she had to endure. Her defense against psychotherapeutic efforts was very rigid. Although she put on some weight through the prescribed intravenous supply, she remained fixated to her hunger disease.

This patient, who even in her early childhood received her father's appreciation only after proper achievements, and who had a mother whom she—like her father—did not accept, was unable to reach a healthy female identification. She remained hungry in her need to be accepted emotionally by her father, and in her unconscious desire to identify with a mother who is respected. The patient remained emotionally empty and was unable to put her narcissism into her femininity. Through a learning process, she had reached near perfection in showing her misery. She was fixated to her hunger disease, perhaps not the least because in this way she was able to get the attention of the nurses and doctors, and at the same time was able to escape the world of demands and failures in her home.

As the example of this anorectic patient shows, the purest of the hunger diseases, anorexia nervosa, has a very questionable prognosis, not only because the "hunger" is such that it can never be appeased, but also because the people concerned have gone through a learning process of incorrect problem-solving behavior, i.e., escape strategy. This patient illustrates that the "addiction to thinness" (the literal translation of the German term *Magersucht*) freed her from facing up to the role of an adult woman. The secondary illness gain (Freud, 1916/1917) of these patients lies in the attention they receive because of their suffering, even to the extent that they risk endangering their lives. Although Brand and Gensicke (1980) as well as Schütze (1980) report preponderantly favorable results of their treatment directed toward behavior and communication (5 out of 7 patients), the majority of publications in the literature indicate a rather doubtful prognosis.

As Stierlin (1980) states, anorexia nervosa is not a frequent disease. Three to five out of 100,000 persons are affected. Its prevalence, however, seems to be increasing. Anorexia nervosa is found predominantly in young females of 12 to 15 years and almost exclusively in those from the well-educated middle and upper classes. People who have suffered from true hunger because of a shortage of money do not generally suffer from anorexia nervosa. This extreme emaciation appears to be willful, an expression of "a bitterly and defiantly led hunger strike where sooner or later one's own life is risked" (Stierlin). And yet we do not get the impression that those who are suffering from anorexia nervosa are particularly free in their decisions. The "ascetic remains a prisoner of the needs he fights against: He has to think constantly of food and of weight reduction and remains possessed thereof" (Stierlin, 1980). Hilde Bruch (1978) deals, among other things, with the question of whether the increase in anorexia nervosa over the last years could also be linked to the fact that women have more freedom nowadays to develop their talents and their capacities than in previous years and decades. The choice between various possibilities gives them the impression of having to do something special. They are also expected to date young men much earlier than the case used to be. A girl who does not act accordingly is considered an outsider. As Hilde Bruch (1978) states, anorexia nervosa often begins after a film presentation or a lecture on sexual education, or after a presentation in school suggesting that girls do something they are apparently not yet ready to do. Bruch assumes three realms of psychic malfunctions to be present before the outbreak of the disease:

1) severe disturbances in the body image, i.e., in the way adolescent girls see themselves;

2) misinterpretations of internal and external stimuli, especially in the perception of the hunger experience;

3) a paralyzing feeling of being helpless and incapable of changing anything in life. The obstinate desire to control the body has to be seen against the background of the feeling of helplessness.

Hilde Bruch (1978) bases her observations on 70 anorectic patients (60 females and 10 males). The picture of the illness she gives is based on the knowledge gathered during psychotherapy with these patients. She stresses that each anorexia nervosa patient believes in her heart that her basic personality is damaged, that she is not good enough, and that all her endeavors are aimed at hiding the fatal "stain." The patients are convinced that other people observe them in a disapproving way.

It results therefore also from Hilde Bruch's research (1978) that these patients, both male and female, received too little self-strength and confirmation of their own value in their early childhood. They are uneasy about themselves and belittle themselves constantly. That their suffering manifests itself in puberty may be linked to the fact that the development toward becoming a woman or a man takes place more intensely and faster during this period. It is not by chance that these narcissistically very seriously damaged people in need of great attention and care do not come to terms with themselves in puberty.

As our case report shows, and as Hilde Bruch (1978) sets forth in her book, it is not easy to treat anorectic patients. They are very obstinate and almost possessed by the feeling of having gained control over their problems through their behavior. The demonstrative physical presentation of their hunger gives evidence to their attempt at compensation by means of a grandiose self. They entertain the illusion of having defeated their physical needs. With certain patients, the anorexia reveals itself in bulimic attacks followed by vomiting. Harju and Fried (1981) speak of "dysorexia," having observed in patients—and their families—this alternation of anorexia and bulimia (see also the chapter on "Bulimia"). A number of these patients take laxatives secretly in order to remain thin. At first, anorectics may accept the interpretations a therapist gives them, but in time they give one the impression—as Hilde Bruch (1978) correctly states—that it means nothing to them. Even in their childhood they were able to adapt themselves to life with their parents without being really touched. Patients with anorexia nervosa demand an immense effort on the part of the therapist. The signs of change are often very difficult to recognize, but they have to be recognized and applauded by the therapist in order to help the patients to overcome their hunger ideology. Only when these patients are convinced of the therapist's unconditional human participation and benevolent attention, and only after having experienced that nothing can keep the therapist away—neither their aggressiveness nor their pseudocooperative behavior—can they be led away from their "hunger disease."

The prognosis is serious, and there is a danger that the people concerned may die from some accompanying disease or from suicide—or from an action with suicidal character, for example, taking an overdose of sleeping pills. Spontaneous recoveries, however, do occur, though the basic psychodynamic pattern usually remains (Mester, 1981).

Some have tried to bring anorexia patients together with very severely ill persons, for example, cancer patients in a terminal state, in order to show them how much they are playing with their life and endangering it. Despite the fact that such a method may lead to increased food intake and may sometimes even convince the patients that their "hunger strike" can have dangerous implications, we should recall that such a treatment strategy will never heal the damaged self-identity. These patients, who often reject themselves, as mentioned, need our complete therapeutic attention. If they are only forced to confront life again by being brought together with cancer patients, they will continue to suffer deeply from "hunger." Nothing in their deficient self will have changed—neither their narcissistic deficit nor their need for an indestructible, unhindered, convincing human empathy stemming from their early life history.

Anorectic patients are afraid of completely "devouring" any object they encounter in their "hunger" for love and attention. The impressive image of hunger they present is meant to motivate their fellow human beings to give them the desired care. Their "hunger ideology" guarantees, on the one hand, constant attention by their social environment (and by the therapist), and on the other hand, it leads to anxiety-provoking tendencies of incorporation and taking possession.

These tendencies can also be observed in the above-mentioned bulimic attacks, whereby these patients afterwards return to the defense mechanism of emaciation. The hunger ideology thus serves as a defense mechanism against their excessive tendency to incorporate and to take possession of objects. With Melanie Klein (1935) we can say that, similar to depressives, these patients long for the total object—while at the same time doing their utmost to free themselves of such tendencies, since, in the bottom of their heart, they know that in the moment of incorporation or possession the object stops being an object to that individual. If such a person succeeds in entering into a therapeutic contact, it is important that the doctor or the psychologist show the patient, on the one hand, that s/he stands behind the patient unconditionally, but on the other hand make it clear that under no circumstances will s/he accept being integrated totally into the patient's world.

Hilde Bruch (1978) emphasizes that a program for weight increase should be established by an internist or pediatrician "in a good, open cooperation with a psychiatrist." Otherwise, patients might be tempted to play off one against the other, thus having recourse to the method they used at home by playing off the mother against the father. Mutual understanding and a good contact with the nurses and the dieticians is necessary. Establishing an adequate framework for the nourishment program is of more importance than the details of the respective meals.

Treatment of these patients at home is possible only if the parents' anxiety level is not too high and if they too are under treatment. Thomae (1961) and Mester (1981) emphasized the correlation between anorexia and family dynamics.

Many anorectics become frightened of eating solid food, spending hour after hour eating the smallest imaginable quantity; or they refuse to eat anything at all. It can therefore be helpful to prescribe a protein-rich liquid preparation.

Feeding anorectics artificially does not have only positive effects, but corresponds also to the desire of these patients for self-punishment, especially if they are fed through a gastrotube. The intravenous supply of life-preserving substances, however, can be vital for the people concerned: It avoids arguments, on the one hand, and any betterment in the nourishing situation appears as a *medical* problem. Whatever feeding procedure is chosen, indulgent, empathetic psychotherapy under psychoanalytic conditions is necessary in order to tackle the basic narcissistic problems.

As mentioned earlier, behavior therapy approaches have also been tried whereby the persons concerned were rewarded or punished depending on whether they had eaten or not. In behavior therapy terms, this means giving a positive or negative reinforcement. A weight increase is rewarded—positively reinforced—and a weight loss punished—negatively reinforced. As Hilde Bruch (1978) correctly states, enthusiasm for a behavior modification is today not what it was some years ago. Weight increase achieved in this way usually lasts only a short period of time. In our experience, it is necessary to treat these patients with individual psychotherapy on a long-term basis. At the same time, one should include the family in the psychotherapy program, if possible, since a pathological interactional pattern regularly occurs in the family (Harju and Fried, 1981) and is in part the cause, in part the result of the anorexia—a fight concerning the food intake behavior of the patient. Yet one also has to keep in mind that the patient's dependency on the family should not be increased from what it already is. One explicit aim of psychotherapy is to lead patients, through a process of maturation, to an increased distance and a detachment from the family.

❖Bulimia nervosa

Bulimics are people who stayed "hungry" during early childhood or later on. Especially during puberty do they suffer from this early lack of love and attention, first because they cannot identify themselves with the role of an adult woman, and second because they do not receive the unquestioning sympathy and loving care they expect in their encounters with representatives of the opposite sex. Bulimics are mostly female adolescents or younger or medium-aged adult women who suffer from uncontrollable binge eating, and who tend to rid themselves of the incorporated food by self-induced vomiting. Binge eating occurs regularly whenever the people concerned have, on the one hand, collected enough frustrating emotional experiences and, on the other hand, when they are especially determined to stop their eating orgies. They eat their food stocks at home and stop only when they have nothing left. This can lead to a senseless intake of food, and they end this devouring of food only when they feel their swollen abdomen and suffer from unpleasant and bothersome feelings of fullness. Yet they fear gaining weight, and after the eating orgy stick a finger or the whole hand into their throat to induce vomiting, whereby sometimes this can go so far as to hurt their finger or hand. Occasionally, they even use a tool to provoke vomiting and thereby hurt their pharynx. Their desperation about their eating can become so intensive that they consider committing suicide.

Maja Langsdorff (1986) writes impressively about, as she calls it, "this secret addiction of eating an awful lot," whereby she points out—as do others (e.g., E. and H. A. Klessmann, 1988)—that bulimia in fact always represents "bulimarexia," that is, bulimia combined with anorexia (see the chapter on "Anorexia"). As Langsdorff rightly states, this addiction is still seen today as the result of loss of self-control. She writes: "The layman does not recognize the real hunger behind the exaggerated need to eat. Specialists are having a hard time revealing the apparent greediness as a real obsession, so that the illness itself—concealed by the people concerned—is irresponsibly misjudged." She says that bulimarexia is metaphorically speaking a "consuming hunger." Such women are hungry for meaning, tasks and recognition, love, feelings and a deeper sense in their lives. In the author's view not the body is hungry but the soul. Here, however, I would like to remark critically the inappropriate distinction between *psyche* and *soma*: Whoever has suffered from a long-lasting emotional and cognitive deficiency experience during childhood is hungry not only for love and (emotional) "nourishment," but at the same time for "food" in a physical and psychological sense. Women who suffer from bulimia and binge eat desire not only fusion with the objects in their fantasy, they also desire to incorporate and to take possession of these objects. They want to become at one with the objects and by that to be able to "experience" them. But this taking into possession and incorporation causes them to lose such objects all the more. An object they have taken in this way loses its object character. Even the knowledge of having incorporated so many objects makes them in the end indigestible and unacceptable, especially if obesity results, which would even further impair their ideals of womanliness and their feelings connected with it—which are only rudimentary anyway because of their growing up without proper love.

It is not easy to say why bulimia or bulimarexia as well as anorexia occur preponderantly among young women. We might suppose that mothers have greater difficulties giving their young daughters than their sons the love that is essential for healthy development. Or we might assume that, especially today with the expected adaptation of the sexes toward each other, it is difficult for women to transmit to their daughters an image of true womanhood. Thus, it may very easily come to an impaired feminine identity in the daughters. One should also consider that in today's society esthetics still play a more important role for women than for men. Of course, also the male sex has ideal notions of its own body image, but the latitude of these ideas is wider than for women, who do not like to be out of line with the modern ideal of slimness. If a woman is insecure in her self-esteem, she will—much more than a man—tend to adapt herself excessively to the normative ideas of society to fit the ideal dimensions and forms of a modern woman.

A 34-year-old woman, wife of an architect, came to the Basel University Psychiatric Outpatient Clinic on the advice of her family doctor. She reported suffering from recurrent nausea since her marriage at age 21. The symptoms increased particularly during her eight pregnancies. After her last delivery, a hysterectomy was done because she suffered from chronic genital bleeding. Since then she had been unable to stop the nausea. Again and again she ate so much food that she had to vomit afterwards. The patient had gone through an anorexia phase at the age of 17. After having moved to Japan, she experienced a total recovery, though later she always had to vomit several times a day after eating. Sometimes she had good days. During the first session in the Outpatient Department, she explained that during meals she loses all control over her food intake and afterwards has to free herself of it. The patient weighed slightly over 40 kg and was 168 cm in height. Her husband as well as her parents and a friend of hers know about her illness, but behave somewhat helplessly and imprudently. A year before consulting the Outpatient Department she was in a sanatorium, where she had been treated with antidepressants, but this therapy was not successful. At the time of her first consultation, she was not taking any medicines.

The patient reported having grown up in a city as the second of three sisters. Her father, a businessman, traveled a lot and openly had a girlfriend. Her parents' marriage had been full of tension. She had a bad relationship with her mother since she never felt accepted by her. Her father had forced her to go through all the educational steps he expected of her: He made her decide either to attend business training or to become a dental assistant. She chose the latter. But after her training, she moved, as mentioned, to Japan, and upon returning passed the exams to enter the university.

Her husband is almost never at home, he works a lot and cares little for her and the family. Lately, she feels on the verge of decompensation. She is sick of everything and mainly has the feeling of missing out on life. Her husband has no interest whatsoever in undergoing therapy. He tells her she can feel guilty alone, and that he cannot give her love. Her four children—four further pregnancies were not carried to term— are a big strain to her.

This patient, who received the necessary love and care for healthy development neither from her mother nor from her father, and who was only expected to satisfy the parental standards of performance, painfully feels—especially since she has children herself—that she is not getting enough attention from her husband. Because of the deficient development of her self during childhood, today she has little self-assertion and is very much in need of love. In a first phase—that of anorexia—she tried to show publicly her affective need by denying food and creating emaciation. In a second phase, in repeated attacks, she "took possession" of the available food at hand and incorporated it into her body. She unconsciously expected a narcissistic reinforcement from the objects incorporated or taken possession of— now that they had become a part of herself and had lost their object character as described above. After an attack of binge eating, she felt an unbearable feeling of satiety—but no satisfaction. In addition, she struggled with frustrating experiences in her marriage as well as with her ideal of womanliness centering on being slim. One can easily understand how in this situation the patient stayed empty in her self.

In patients who consulted the Basel Psychiatric Outpatient Clinic in the years 1986-1988 because of bulimia, Keel (1988) observed—in correspondence with the literature (Paul et al., 1987; Mitchell et al., 1985; and others)—that the beginning of the illness occurred mostly in late adolescence. The 275 patients Mitchell and coworkers examined were on average 24.8 years old with an average length of the illness of 7 years. The authors report a number of abnormal eating behaviors: binge eating (10%), laxative abuse (60.6%), diuretic abuse (33.1%), chewing and regurgitation of food (64.5%), alcohol and drug as well as social problems (each 33%). Often a short period of being over-weight or an anorectic phase preceded the bulimic symptoms.

How big the hunger of these bulimic—or anorectic—patients for objects is can also be seen in the thefts observed among the people concerned, which in the author's opinion do not corre-spond, as Gerlinghoff and Backmund (1987) suppose, to compen-satory actions of sexual instinct (as in kleptomania), but result from the unconscious desire to take possession of objects and/or to incorporate them into a deeply felt narcissistic emptiness, as Keller et al. (1981) have written. This taking possession of objects can also be observed in depressives: Gerlinghoff and Backmund (1987) observed that 15 of 63 bulimic patients had committed thefts.

These people have an enormous longing for objects, but even more so for human warmth, recognition and attention. What they unconsciously want is basically not to increase their material possessions, but to fuse with the objects in order to reinforce their weak selves.

> A woman of 54 years has been in psychotherapy with the author for 16 years. She is the mother of two children and married to a man of the same age who is still oedipally fixed to his deceased mother. This woman suffers from no longer being admired as much as in the past—by her husband and by other men on the street. She feels unloved, and especially when she has this impression very strongly, she goes to the refrigerator and begins eating without consideration. At the age of 51 she weighs 68 kg at a height of 172 cm. She used to weigh 54-58 kg. She could reduce her weight by fasting, but this devouring of food was often her only pleasure, though afterwards it brought sorrow and despair and left her as empty as before.

This woman has depressive tendencies in her paternal family. Her paternal grandfather was depressive, and his brother committed suicide at an unknown age. Also, the mother has been treated psychiatrically because of a late depression. As a child, the patient was very timid and felt rejected compared with her younger brother, who was always encouraged very much. At the age of 12, she had her menarche. After finishing her schooling with good results, she worked as a secretary and was appreciated because of her proficiency. At the age of 28, she married the man mentioned above. Her mother-in-law often stayed with them although she had a house of her own in another country. On the surface, the couple got along well together, but on the inside the patient often felt empty. Her bulimic attacks began around the age of 50.

As is obvious with this patient, people who have a tendency toward bulimia did not as young children have the experience of being accepted as they were and of receiving loving attention, either because of the missing care or because of overprotection on the part of the parents. Or the child suffered from having to live according to the parents' expectations. The addicted intake of— edible—objects in the sense of taking possession of as well as incorporation of may be seen in all bulimics as an unconscious— and unsuccessful—attempt to reinforce a self that was insufficiently built up in early childhood or later on. Those concerned, mostly females, thus suffer from a narcissistic disorder. A part of them display a rather consistent ego and are not severely damaged in their ability to master reality, except that they suffer from feelings of insufficiency, sometimes have dull-depressive moods, and show compensatory tendencies through discrete feelings of grandiosity, a desire for fusion with objects as well as a tendency toward mirror relationships and transferences. They are people who suffer from *narcissistic personality disorders* according to Kohut (1971/77) or *narcissistic neuroses* (Battegay, 1977). The other part of them are borderline personalities, who are more deeply disturbed and who, having an ego prone to fragmentation, were hardly able or completely unable to perceive the affection they received or unconsciously set up defenses against it—even when they were offered appropriate care and love in their early childhood.

Mitchell et al. (1986) found that there was no family history of depression in the first-grade relatives in 164 (59.6%) of the 275 patients they examined. In the other 111 (40.4%) patients, at least one of the first-grade relatives suffered from a monopolar or bipolar depressive disorder. Furthermore, the study showed that the patients with a positive family history for affective disorders differed only little from the others with respect to binge eating, duration of illness, and age of onset of treatment. The patients with a positive family history for affective disorders, however, were treated more often for depressions. The group with a positive family history was not judged as being more depressive than the one without this familial disposition.

The relationship between depression and bulimia lies in the fact that all studies show that patients who have a tendency toward bulimia often also suffer from the depressive symptoms typical of narcissistic disorders. Since depressive states correspond to a more or less total narcissistic depletion (Battegay, 1986), it can be said that those concerned especially feel this intolerable inner emptiness that forces them into—for them—critical situations in which they are thrown back on themselves and their narcissistic vacuum, for example, evenings after work alone at home—filling their narcissistic void with food.

In treating this disorder, it is first important not to hinder them from eating. Through the therapy they should gain self-confidence as well as the ability to control their food intake so that they may experience success. According to our experiences, the prognosis varies depending on whether they have a narcissistic personality disorder (narcissistic neurosis) or a borderline condition as the basis of bulimia. With the latter, the insufficient mastering of reality and, as a result, the impairment of communication lead to their repeatedly feeling narcissistically injured, and because of this they develop a tendency toward binge eating. Therapy may often last for years. With patients with narcissistic personality disorders, on the other hand, it is much easier to reach the therapeutic goal, because the patients generally develop good compliance and cooperate well with the proposed treatment.

All bulimics need, on the one hand, the therapist's unreserved attention, but on the other hand, they must continually be made aware of their pattern of solving problems and their useless attempts at filling their narcissistic void with food. They have to be cognitively trained to recognize their behavior pattern, so that, in frustrating situations, they are able to stop their desire to incorporate and take possession of food, by avoiding it and distracting themselves consciously. It is essential that they have at home only the minimal amount of food necessary for one day's time. Furthermore, they must, as Habermas and Müller (1986) emphasize, follow an exact eating schedule with three meals and the allowed amount of carbohydrates and keep a diary of food intake. It is also important that these patients structure their day so as to reduce the danger of feeling their narcissistic emptiness.

The recommended treatment of bulimics often lies not only in individual psychotherapy, but also in group psychotherapy. Brotman and coworkers (1988) worked with therapy groups of 14 bulimic female patients between 19 and 35 years (average 24.3 years) and an average duration of illness of 3.5 years before coming for treatment. If necessary, they also were given parallel individual psychotherapy and antidepressive drugs. Under this therapy, 12 patients experienced a remission. It appears that patients who were also diagnosed as suffering from an affective or a personality disorder responded less positively to the therapy and needed treatment longer than patients who showed only symptoms of bulimia.

The results of group therapy with bulimia patients are encouraging, as other reports (Oesterheld et al., 1987) and the experiences at the Basel University Psychiatric Outpatient Clinic (Keel, 1988) show. According to Oesterheld et al., different models of group psychotherapy lead to a reduction of the symptoms in 52-57% of the cases with respect to binge eating, vomiting, or episodes of eating and vomiting. Most authors report a reduction of symptoms in the range of 70%. The methods of examination, however, seem to be so different that no reliable conclusion for the true degree of therapeutic success can be made. Also, it is problematic to calculate a percentage of reduction in symptoms that have often been evaluated only vaguely and subjectively. Rather, it is more reliable to refer the results of treatment to the single patient. For example, Stevens and Salisbury (1984) report that 6 out of 8 patients they treated with group psychotherapy were free of binge eating at a follow-up 10 months after beginning the treatment. Brisman and Siegel (1985) also report good results of group psychotherapy with bulimics, emphasizing that the patients were reinforced by the treatment group in their ego functions. In this context, on the basis of his experience at the Basel Psychiatric Outpatient Department, the author would rather think that those who take part in a treatment group of bulimics experience the necessary support for their selves and for their narcissism. Then the ego too can be better invested narcissistically. In addition, as was also observed in the group of obese

27

patients (see following chapter), these patients are better able to fight their false problem-solving patterns together than alone.

❖Obesity

As already mentioned in the introduction to the chapter "Anorexia nervosa," "food-intake behavior" is a very complex process that not only has a psychological basis, but is also regulated by the neuronal and metabolic system. Hetherington and Ranson (1940) have already shown (see above in the chapter "Anorexia") that bilateral lesions in the ventromedial hypothalamus of rats lead to a weight increase. The primary effect of the lesion seems to be to cause them to eat in excess, so that they develop hyperphagia. Morley (1980), therefore, pointed to the ventromedial hypothalamus as the satiation center, and to the ventrolateral part thereof as the food-intake center. As trials have shown (Morley, 1980), cerebral transmitters regulate food-intake behavior. The hypothalamic nuclei mentioned are under the constant influence of these transmitters. From trials with rats—though not undisputed (Wallace et al. 1981)—the conclusion was drawn that the circulating immunoreactive beta-endorphine has essentially a stimulating effect on food intake. Naloxone, which operates antagonistically on it, apparently hinders the influence of the beta-endorphine and leads to emaciation in the animals (Margules et al., 1978). Morley and Levine (1980) have determined that stress-induced eating in rats is obtained through the endorphines. These stress-induced eating reactions of rats were stopped by the opiate antagonist Naloxone. It would thus seem that—endogenous—endorphine contributes essentially to the control of food-intake behavior.

McCloy and McCloy (1979) formed the hypothesis that obese persons become addicted to stimulations provoked by endogenous opiates. Pradalier et al. (1980) tried to confirm this theory by examining obese individuals. If this supposition proves to be correct, it would be possible to understand why there was a relationship between obesity and sensitivity to pain: Obese woman were found to have an increased sensitivity to pain (Pradalier et al., 1980).

However, not only endogenous opiates influence hunger, but other transmitter substances of the brain do so as well, for example, serotonin, dopamine, and norepinephrine. They all stand in a mutual relationship with endogenous morphine. Morley (1980) has pointed out that the satiety center in the ventromedial

29

hypothalamus is under positive serotonin control. If serotonin is mobilized via any substances, it leads to anorexia; if serotonin antagonists are given intraventricularly, this effect is stopped and hyperphagia occurs; if norepinephrine is injected into the rat's ventromedial hypothalamus, food intake is stimulated. Dopamine also seems to have a stimulating effect on food intake, especially on the lateral hypothalamus. All these transmitters stand in a mutual relationship to each other and act partly in the same sense and partly antagonistically on the above-mentioned brain centers regulating food intake.

Hyperphagia followed by obesity because of damage in the ventromedial hypothalamus has been observed not only in rats, but also in other rodents as well as in cats, monkeys, and humans. The ventromedial hypothalamus syndrome changes over the course of time. Immediately after the lesion is made, the rats eat enormously large meals—and they take food more frequently, especially during the daytime, although rats normally eat at night. At the end of the first week after the lesion, the size of the meals decreases, but the amount of the food is still higher than usual. During this hyperphagia period, the rat's weight increases rapidly, basically the result of an increase in fat. Brobeck et al. (1943) called this phase of hyperphagia and that of the rapid weight increase the *dynamic phase* of the syndrome. Approximately 1 to 2 months after the lesion to the ventromedial hypothalamus, the size of the meals and the frequency of food intake are almost normalized—although food intake during the daytime is still more frequent than before the lesion. The reduced food intake leads to a reduced weight increase until it reaches a normal increase of the body weight. The rats' weight, however, remains much higher than it should be. The above-mentioned authors call this period of normal food intake and normal weight increase (on the basis of the existing obesity) the *static phase* of the syndrome. Discontinuation of the hyperphagia during this phase is not the result of a recovery of the normal neuronal food-intake control during the month following the lesion to the ventromedial part of the hypothalamus: The hyperphagia appears again if weight loss is provoked in the corresponding rats. If rats are made fat before the lesion is made in the ventromedial hypothalamus, they do not show hyperphagia (Hoebel & Teitelbaum, 1966), though they do keep their excessive weight. Therefore, it looks as though the rats are eating sufficiently in this static phase of the ventromedial hypothalamus syndrome in order to keep up their excessive body weight. But they are no longer hyperphagic.

The fact that hyperphagia correlates reciprocally with obesity after a lesion to the ventromedial hypothalamus is one of the reasons why Kennedy (1953) postulated that body fat should have a restrictive influence on food-intake behavior. Hyperphagia also depends, by the way, more so than is normally expected, on taste, that is, on both good and bad tastes.

The lipostatic hypothesis is based on the observation that in adult mammals the quantity of the depot fat in relation to the body weight remains stable up to old age (Kennedy, 1953). This relationship does not exist in rats during development. Kennedy (1953) interpreted this correlation between depot fat and body weight in adult mammals to mean that body fat hinders food intake in the adult animal. This lipostatic hypothesis was tested experimentally by measuring the effect on food intake after increasing or decreasing the quantity of body fat. If depot fat and body weight were increased, either by giving a daily dose of insulin (Hoebel & Teitelbaum, 1966) or by excessive feedings via gastrotube (Cohn & Joseph, 1962), then food intake was decreased; if insulin application and the feeding by gastrotube ceased, food intake remained partially hindered until body weight and depot fat became normal again. Also, the contrary was observed when body weight and depot fat were decreased: The animals ate more until they again regained the previously lost body weight. Hypotheses were postulated as to how the ventromedial hypothalamic syndrome is connected to the interrelation between body fat and food intake. For example, Kennedy (1953) suggested that the ventromedial hypothalamus lesion reduced the sensitivity of the neuronal system, which controls the food intake with respect to the inhibiting effect of body fat. Thus, these animals eat more. But if the fat quantity were sufficient, it would enable them to overcome this insensitivity, food intake would be inhibited, and the hyperphagia would end. Hirsch and Han (1969) showed that the body fat of rats with ventromedial hypothalamic syndrome is characterized by a normal amount of very large cells. Results of other researchers also indicate that enlarged fat cells form the basis for the hyposensitive inhibition of the food intake.

Other factors are, of course, also decisive for food-intake quantity, such as the temperature of the environment—more is eaten during the cold than during the warm season. But also an emotional tenseness or a relaxed "atmosphere" is decisive for food-intake behavior. The effects, however, differ: Some eat a great deal when they are tense and sad, some eat less, whereas to date it is unknown exactly why these different behaviors exist.

It is certainly also important how quickly one eats, how many times one chews, how full the stomach is, and how quickly the stomach content is emptied.

Mayer and Bates (1952) established a glucostatic hypothesis and related glucose metabolism to food-intake behavior. Their hypothesis consists of three major points:

1) Glucostatic food-intake control acts on the basis of the glucose concentration in the blood caused by the individual meals.

2) Glucose utilization by the brain, especially by the ventromedial zone of the hypothalamus, is the critical parameter of glucose turnover which controls food-intake behavior.

3) Food intake and utilized glucose are reversely proportional to one another, so that reduced glucose consumption stimulates food intake, while increased glucose consumption restricts food intake.

Brobeck (1979) came to the conclusion that—until newer experiments prove the contrary—it has to be assumed (1) that the brain is stimulated through reduced glucose consumption, (2) that this fact is based on a metabolic emergency reaction, and (3) that the circumstances mentioned nevertheless have nothing to do with food-intake stimulation under normal conditions. Russek (1975) mentions that liver glucose metabolism rather than the central nervous glucose metabolism should control the food intake.

In this context, we cannot consider all the other theories in detail. They do allow us, however, to recognize the abundance of existing research results that all need to be treated further. They also show us how closely the somatic substrate is connected with the psychological situation of food intake in animal trials. Still, we cannot draw any direct conclusions from the animal trials for humans, although we do have reason to assume that human food-intake behavior is codetermined by manifold physiological, psychological, climatic as well as further factors.

Let us now turn to the emotional aspect of obesity, whereby we have to be aware that our knowledge is ever in need of updating. One day it may be possible to find out exactly how the physical processes are connected with the emotional and cognitive spheres.

Obese individuals are obviously persons who, because of their "hunger disease," tend to eat excessively or to utilize the food more than is optimal. For the most part, they eat very quickly, hastily, so that their hunger feeling continually lags behind. They therefore still feel hungry although objectively they have already "filled up their stomach." Their eating style often reminds one of greediness. They continue to eat even when the enjoyable appetite has disappeared and only the tendency to incorporate an object and/or to take possession of it—the "hunger"—remains.

Perls (1947/1969) thinks that certain adults treat their solid food as if it were liquid food that can be swallowed in big gulps. Such persons, the author thinks, are always impatient. They have not developed any interest in consuming solid food. Their impatience seems to be coupled with greediness and the incapacity to attain true satisfaction. Perls (1947/1969) is apparently speaking of the greedy swallowing of objects leading to the objects no longer being perceived as such. These individuals are unable to obtain true satisfaction through food, though they nevertheless hope to experience contentment and thus tend to eat more and more. Obese people are therefore not necessarily individuals who enjoy their food; rather, they eat large quantities in haste, because they hope—in vain—for being truly satiated just once.

It is known that the manner and the amount of food intake in earliest childhood are decisive not only for the learning process with respect to later food-intake behavior, but also for the factors determining the needs of the cells (for fat) and their quantity in the body. Individuals who have gone through a learning process directed toward excessive food intake are also—more or less—physically fixated on it. These people have been trained at the psychological and the somatic level to feel hungry.

Individuals who have gone through a learning process of overeating are less able than others to resist external temptations. Like any addicts, obese people tend to be fascinated by objects more quickly and then to incorporate them or take possession thereof. If they have swallowed an object once, they have to perform this process repeatedly, since an object incorporated in this way ceases to be an object. Thus, such people remain insatiated and insatiable. They have to absorb continuously the object of their addiction—food—in order to strengthen their insufficient self and give themselves more social "weight," especially in their own eyes. In their own fantasy these individuals have a self-image that is linked with their obesity. Losing weight may mean losing social weight, importance and maybe charm—but it may also mean that they might become more attractive and would thus be forced to deal with their environment: to lose that fatty layer around them that keeps them from having closer contact with their surroundings.

In the language of Melanie Klein (1940), obese people are constantly seeking an object that will reinforce them and increase their significance. In their childhood these individuals rarely experienced the loving, caring and reinforcing object that is of such importance to healthy development. And without this they have not been able to acquire adequate self-representation and have developed only a poor object representation. Their whole life long they look for self-confirmation and fusion with an object that might help them to overcome this deficiency once and for all. They are never satisfied with their tendency toward fusion with an object, and they therefore tend to incorporate new objects and/or to take possession of them—insatiably and continuously.

Pudel and Meyer (1981) have stated, among other things, that obese people depend much more than other people on external stimuli linked with food intake. While the hunger feeling is generally regulated by internal signals (e.g., the filling of the stomach), obese people apparently react much more to external stimuli. The two authors quote Katz (1932), who formulated a two-component hunger theory. His experiments—mainly with chickens—strongly proved that food intake is regulated not only by an organism's physiological state, but also by the external situation encountered. Schachter et al. (1962) were repeatedly able to differentiate the food behavior of obese and normal-weight individuals. Based on Katz's (1932) two-component theory, they found that the specific food behavior of obese persons is more independent of internal, physiological stimuli and thus more dependent on external stimuli linked with food intake. If obese people are given a second serving, their feeling of hunger is stimulated by the visible food, and they eat even if they have already consumed enough. Psychodynamically expressed, this means that the visibility of edible objects stimulates them such that they incorporate them or take possession thereof. Their eyes and their damaged self are insatiable. This observation suggests that these people wish to experience the complete object, but that they at best experience an object as an unstable partial object. They remain unsatiated.

A 43-year-old woman reported that her father was earlier a manager in a company and suffered a social decline because of his alcohol dependence. She said that during her childhood the father was tender and open, and that she was used to having a close relationship with him. On the other hand, when drunk he suddenly became very brutal. When her father came home drunk, her mother used to flee the home together with the patient's older sister, leaving her alone with the father. Sometimes she succeeded in calming him down; often, however, she herself had to go out in her nightgown to the nearest police station to escape her father's aggressive and destructive outbursts. She registered him with a medical health center for alcoholics so that he could be taken care of. In the family, she developed both feelings of responsibility and feelings of guilt because of her anger about each interruption of family harmony. Even as a small child she had to assume household obligations such as shopping, washing up and helping with meals so that she often arrived too late at kindergarten. Because the family was very poor, her mother, who was very tight with money, had to go to work. From the daughter she expected support, yet she did not further the daughter, but rather often rejected her because of her special relationship with the father. The patient, on the one hand, had feelings of hatred toward her mother, and on the other hand, she had a great unfulfilled—and unfulfillable—desire to be cared for, to simply be dependent on someone.

When sitting at the table, the family experienced moments of harmony, so that the patient took hope again and gained confidence. At meals the family had very pleasurable and joyful relationships. When she remembered these moments, she was able to get in touch with herself again, in her fantasy turning each cup of coffee and each piece of bread into a feast. Needless to say, the patient tried to compensate any wrong by eating. Following primary and secondary school, she—always obese from childhood onwards—went through an apprenticeship to become a corsetiere. During the final examination she met her later husband, a painter. The first years of marriage were overshadowed by great financial problems, particularly because the family had taken out loans from banks and had to repay them by installment. The loans were necessary because of the high demands of the patient, but also because of the additional financial obligations occurring during and after the birth of two sons, and because of her illnesses. Her husband directed his interest more and more toward handball and did not fulfill his wife's wishes to be cared for. Very severe marriage problems occurred, also because of a third (unwanted) pregnancy. In order to make the installment payments, the husband worked till late at night. He finally broke down with a slipped disc, but after a while was able to work again. The patient came to the Basel Psychiatric Outpatient Clinic for therapy when the eldest son had detached himself from the family and a nurse friend of the family who had supported them up till then became infirm.

The history of this obese woman shows that she was basically still "hungry" and still looking for the warmth and safety and the emotional "nourishment" she had not received during childhood. Very early on she had had to take on a responsibility she was not up to, so that she later tended all the more to develop a narcissistic-fusionary and an oral-incorporative relationship with her surroundings—none of which was conscious to her. She had only a rudimentary relationship with the world of her feelings and suffered from alexithymia, which Sifneos (1973) described as being typical for all patients with psychosomatic disorders. This woman was constantly looking for the "good" object, but in the moment in which she "swallowed" it or fused with it, the object turned out to be "bad," much as Melanie Klein (1932) described this phenomenon, since it then no longer existed—as a reinforcing object—in her experience. Obese persons thus often consider the food they have eaten in excess as more or less self-destructive.

Grinker (1953) stressed that it is incorrect to speak only of oral libido in the case of an early fixation to the first months and years of life. He underlines that pleasure in the first phases of development can be obtained from all organs and body zones. The author agrees with this opinion, but would add that not only in the early stages of development does especially the skin determine an individual's boundaries, but already *intra utero* serves for exchange processes with the environment. And after birth and later on it is of extreme importance for the reception of stimuli. A baby that is not loved and is not put to the mother's breast or held to her body, and therefore cannot have tactile contact with her, will tend to take possession of objects insatiably and/or to incorporate them over its whole life span, as has been observed in the above-mentioned patient, in a fusionary-narcissistic and oral-captive manner. It should be added that this patient had, as is often the case, gone through a learning process of using as problem-solving behavior the fusion with objects and/or introduction of the object into her mouth. No sooner had a problem arisen than she began to eat, regardless of the type of question. She developed what is called in German "sad fat." The obesity was an obvious sign of her "hunger disease."

Perhaps the early psychoanalysis put too much emphasis on orality. One could (wrongly) think that it is decisive whether a child was breast-fed or received an artificial product. Obviously, in underdeveloped countries it is not favorable if mothers completely "unlearn" breast-feeding, as the hygienic conditions are usually so poor that the artificial milk given to the babies is often infected. If, however, these mothers were properly educated, this danger could be omitted. In any case, a mother's attention should be drawn to the fact that even when artificial food is given in a bottle, it is the *skin contact* with the small child that is of utmost importance. During breast-feeding, direct mouth contact takes place with the mother's nipple and thus an intimate tactile relationship between child and mother. When the bottle is given, the milk is warmed up to body temperature and a warm contact occurs with the rubber nipple. But that is not sufficient: The child must also have the opportunity to enter into a direct relationship with the mother's body warmth and to have tactile contact with her if the child is not to remain "hungry" for warmth as well as physical and emotional stimulation, which are necessary for the development of a healthy experience of self-esteem and adequate object representation.

For this reason, the author has named the first phase of child development directly after birth and up to about the the 8th or 9th month of life the "tactile-symbiotic phase." In this phase of development, the child needs tactile contact—a fusion or symbiosis with the mother (Mahler, 1968). The zoologist Portmann (1944) stated that human beings enter the world as physiological premature births. In comparison to other primates, a human being is dependant on a "social uterus" for healthy development during the first 9 months of life. If this environment does not function properly—if adequate care is not given—the child's self remains damaged. Yet the child may also be damaged if it is "overfed" with tactile and oral stimuli, that is, if it is overstimulated during this phase or later. But, as mentioned earlier, also if the mother or the parents expect from the child the fulfillment of an ideal development will the child be unable to develop a consistent self, since it is not loved and stimulated as such and receives narcissistic gratifications only when it corresponds to the parental expectations. These children are damaged for their whole lives and desire fusion, "nourishment," taking possession of objects and their incorporation. If children are primarily overstimulated with love and attention, it comes secondarily to a frustration concerning the experience of gratification and care: These children suffer in the long run equally from a narcissistic deficiency. The psychoanalyst Walter Schindler (1968) expressed this when he said that people who have been primarily spoiled are always secondarily frustrated.

Such are the basic and fundamental disturbances in early childhood that seem to be present in the majority of obese people.

Bachofner and Stransky (1977) as well as Stauder (1959) have correctly commented that obesity could today be considered one of the most important nutritional problems. There are, as these authors stress, nearly linear relationships between the degree of obesity and the increasing morbidity from, for the most part, cardiovascular diseases such as arteriosclerosis, myocardial infarction, hypertension, stroke, as well as diabetes mellitus, disturbances of the vertebral column, etc. For this reason, the problem of obesity is important not only because it indicates that an emotional deficiency occurred during early childhood—be it emotional undernourishment, overnournishment with love and stimulation, or "feeding" the child with false expectations with respect to development; it is also a central factor in the prevention of the diseases mentioned and others.

Stunkard and coworkers (1959) examined 25 obese persons at the New York Hospital who were influenced by therapy only marginally. They compared this group with 38 patients without weight problems. It appeared that the obese individuals were prone to eating much more frequently at night than the control group: Of the 25 overweight patients, 16 reported eating excessively at night, whereas none of the 38 persons in the control group did so. The authors noted that especially acute emotional disturbances led to an excess of food intake at night. If these people tried to stop their trip to the refrigerator and their nightly food intake, they became depressive or dysphoric. Apparently they tried to compensate their emotional deficiency, which became apparent especially at night, by means of food intake. It is known from our own experience that narcissistically disturbed persons suffer especially at night from their feelings of loneliness and therefore seek fusion with an object at that time—by incorporation or taking possession—in the hopes of obtaining a reinforcement of their selves.

Stunkard and coworkers (1959) observed that patients with the night-eating syndrome almost always have sleep disturbances and empty their refrigerator at that time. Their insomnia also points to their emotional impairment. From the author's point of view, it can be said that narcissistically disturbed people feel alone especially at night and therefore also suffer from sleep disturbances.

Manfred Bleuler (1952) thought that it is not difficult to understand psychologically the food addiction, the slowness, and the adipose degeneration of obese people in the framework of their personality development. He further underlines, however, that one does have to be cautious and not conclude that obesity is thus only of psychological origin.

In a study comprising 20 female and 20 male obese persons, Freyberger and Strube (1963) tried to determine the motivation behind the increased desire to eat excessively, by means of exploration and psychological tests. They emphasize that the environment has an important impact on the eating patterns of these people. They speak of a "peristatic inducibility" of increased food intake. The increased need to eat, however, is also understood by these authors as an expression of a "substitute gratification" for drives that are not fulfilled otherwise; or, expressed in the language of the comparative behavior research, as a displacement reaction, i.e., an action observed in animals that takes place under certain conditions of inhibition when an activated energy of excitement for a certain drive action is discharged through the track of another drive action.

The authors point out that in order to understand the tendency of these patients toward denial, it is important to recognize such displacement reactions, which often remain preconscious or even totally unconscious to these persons and are perceived only secondarily.

In order to better understand the psychology of obese people on the one hand, and to be able to influence more effectively their food intake behavior on the other hand, a psychotherapy group of obese patients was set up at the Basel University Psychiatric Outpatient Clinic. Group psychotherapy took place under the leadership of a psychiatrist and was for the most part analytically oriented. A once-weekly session of 1 1/2 hours duration was held from March 1976 until May 1978 (88 group sessions). After each session the leader wrote a protocol in which he noted the number of participants, the patients' names and body weight— who were weighed after each session—and the number and kind of interactions, inasmuch as possible. The group moderator regularly visited the weekly supervision seminar of the outpatient department. Two years later, from January 29th to April 6th, 1980, follow-up data were collected in individual single sessions.

So as not to complicate matters further, only female patients were accepted into the group. The patients had come in part spontaneously to the University Psychiatric Outpatient Clinic, and in part they had been sent by their psychiatrists or other doctors. After a first interview with the group leader, these obese patients were proposed for the participation in the group; dates of entry were from 7 March to 25 July 1977. A total of 11 obese female patients became members of the group. During the first (individual) interview of one hour, a psychodynamic as well as a psychiatric diagnosis was formulated. In addition, body weight at the first interview was recorded. Further, the whole history of obesity was registered, including the body weight of the parents and the eating habits of the primal family. Also, general social data were collected.

Table I* lists the psychiatric diagnoses, the initial body weight, the obesity of the parents and, if possible, the approximate begin of obesity in these female patients.

For the follow-up inquiry, the female patients were requested in writing to come to the University Psychiatric Outpatient department for a talk. The following data were gathered during individual sessions: body weight at the time of follow-up inquiry, change in work situation, change in important persons, other life events since leaving the group, psychotherapy or other treatment obtained since the end of group activity, observed diets at the time of inquiry, medicines being taken, retrospective judgment of the group, and judgment of present life situation.

Table II gives an overview of the body weight of the people concerned at the beginning and at the end of the group activity as well as at the follow-up study approximately 2 years after the end of group treatment. The weight with the highest life expectancy was taken as the ideal weight (Stat. Bull. Metrop. Life Insur. Co. 40, Nov./Dec. 1959).

Table III indicates whether the patients were under psychiatric or other treatment, whether they were following a diet, whether they consumed appetite killers, and whether they suffered from any additional somatic disease.

---

*   I wish to thank Hanspeter Lipp, Ursula Miest, Christine Glauser and Udo Rauchfleisch for their valuable help in collecting the required data (Battegay et al., 1981).

Table I. Personal data.

Pat. no.	Year of birth	Diagnosis	Initial bodyweight (kg)	Father obese	Mother obese	Obese since
1	1952	Narcissistic neurosis (Narcissistic Personality Disorder)	115	−	+	early childhood
2	1951	Depressive-narcissistic neurosis	168	+	−	primary school
3	1941	Narcissistic neurosis	97.5	+	−	age 26, after operation
4	1937	Narcissistic neurosis	124	+	+	a baby
5	1943	Depressive neurosis (dysthymic disorder)	103.5			age 23, foreign country
6	1919	Oedipal neurosis	92	+	−	age 26, 1st pregnancy
7	1947	Neurotic infantilism	60.5	+	+	age 25, 1st pregnancy
8	1923	Narcissistic neurosis	91	−	+	age 22, 1st pregnancy
9	1957	Anxiety neurosis	89	+	−	prepuberty
10	1946	Healthy	77.5	+	−	early childhood
11	1914	Narcissistic neurosis	107.5	−	−	age 32, after infectious disease

Table II. Development of body weight.

Pat. no.	Absolute body weight (kg)			Relative overweight (%)		
	Beginning of group psychotherapy (t_1)	End of group psychotherapy (t_2)	Catamnestic examination (t_3)	Beginning of group psychotherapy (t_1)	End of group psychotherapy (t_2)	Catamnestic examination (t_3)
1	115	97	115	80	52	80
2	168	186	190	205	238	245
3	97.5	72	73	52	13	14
4	124	126.5	128	118	122	125
5	103.5	104	97	50	51	41
6	92	78.5	84	70	45	56
7	60.5	52	59	19	2	16
8	91	89.5	94	47	28	52
9	89	78	62	56	37	9
10	77.5	74	80	27	21	31
11	107.5	104	105	111	104	106
Total	1125.5	1061.5	1087	835	713	775
Mean	102.3	96.5	98.8	75.19	64.8	70.5

Table III. Treatment.

Pat. no.	Psychiatric treatment	Other therapies	Diagnosis	Diet	Appetite killer
1	–	–		–	–
2	–	–		yes	–
3	–	yes	art. hypertension	yes	–
4	yes (new)	yes	art. hypertension	yes	–
5	yes (earlier)	yes	psoriasis	–	–
6	–	yes	art. hypertension	yes	–
7	yes (new)	–		yes	–
8	yes (earlier)	yes	state after Lupus erythematodes	yes	–
9	–	–		yes	yes
10	–	–		yes	–
11	–	yes	art. hypertension	yes	–

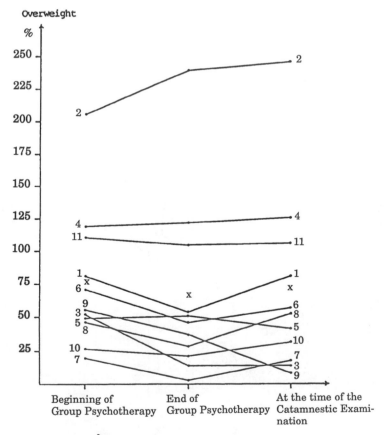

x = mean value

Table IV. Social data.

Pat. no.	Important persons	Working place	Other	Quality of life situation at catamnestic examination
1	marriage better	change of job	stop smoking	happy
2	–	–	–	happy
3	death of friend	change of job	reduction of smoking	neutral
4	–	–	–	happy
5	divorce	–	–	unhappy
6	husband 50% unemployed from myocardial infarction	–	–	unhappy
7	separation, new friend	change of job	move to smaller flat	unhappy
8	father died, husband 50% unemployed	–	–	unhappy
9	marriage	change of profession	–	happy
10	–	–	–	happy
11	–	–	–	neutral

Table V. Evaluation of the group and the leader.

Pat. no.	Group has helped personally	If yes, to what extent?	Behavior of the leader	Disturbances
1	yes	identification	good	one patient with little overweight
2	no		too passive	inhomogeneity of the personalities
3	yes	incentive and rivalry	too passive	not enough dealing with the personality
4	no		good	inhomogeneity concerning the intellectual level
5	no		no comment	own depressivity
6	yes	shame to add weight	too passive	none
7	yes	incentive	too passive	one member with little overweight
8	yes	incentive	good	inhomogeneity concerning the generations
9	no		no comment	personally no confidence
10	yes	control function	too passive	abrupt end of the session because of time
11	yes	incentive	too passive	none

Table IV lists special characteristics of important persons and of the work place, the present experienced quality of life and other social peculiarities.

Table V shows how the patients evaluated the effectiveness of the group and the leader.

The body weight before and immediately after termination of group psychotherapy and at the time of the follow-up inquiry is shown in the graph separately for each patient. Concerning the development of body weight two hypotheses were made:

1) Hypothesis 1: $BW_{t2} - BW_{t1} < 0$

2) Hypothesis 2: $BW_{t3} - BW_{t1} < 0$

The relative body weight conditions are given for each patient separately (in % of overweight).

It can be seen that the mean relative reduction of body weight of the group during group psychotherapy is statistically significant ($p<0.05$). Of 11 patients, 8 reduced their body weight during the treatment, 1 had constant body weight, and 2 showed an increase in body weight. At follow-up, the group still showed a reduction in mean body weight compared with the beginning of treatment. This difference, however, is not significant, i.e., some recidivisms of increased overweight occurred. At follow-up, six of the 11 patients still had reduced body weight compared to that at the beginning of treatment, one had the same weight as before, and four were heavier than before beginning group therapy.

The first hypothesis—that immediately after termination of group psychotherapy the patients would have a mean *decrease* in weight compared with before—was therefore confirmed statistically (t-test). The second hypothesis—that at follow-up the reduction of body weight would remain significant—could not be proven, however.

Thus, we conclude that group psychotherapy with obese patients had an effect on the food intake of the participants. This result is in accordance with the reported experiences by other authors (Dorfman et al., 1959, Kaplan, 1966, Lassiter et al., 1973). The members do not want to do worse than the other participants in the reduction of body weight, so that they observe diet prescriptions better than if they were alone, and the majority lose weight. The reduction of body weight in the group results, first, from the attention, emotional warmth and stimulation these patients—with their narcissistic and/or oral needs—experience in this milieu and lack in their everyday life; second, from the rivalry they experience in reducing their body weight. The effect of group psychotherapy apparently does not last very long, though: The reduction in body weight did not or not equally hold until the time of the follow-up study. The obese persons were apparently not able to introject the group for the weight-reducing effect to remain stable. This is characteristic of individuals suffering from a narcissistic neurosis (narcissistic personality disorder), a depressive neurosis (dysthymia) or a combination thereof. These people need continual attention, emotional warmth and renewed confirmation. Since they do not receive this necessary nourishment in their everyday environment, they relapse into excessive food intake. The objects they swallow and take possession of are no longer present for them and so they have to eat—greedily—once again.

We conclude from these results that a therapy group of obese people should be put at the disposal of these patients for a long period of time, perhaps even lifelong. As in the therapy of all addicts and dependents, they need continual therapeutic availability, the feeling of being protected and cared for. Only if a therapeutic group exists continually for years—and thus a fusion in the patients' fantasy with each other becomes possible—is a long-term compensation of the excessive food intake feasible. The disturbance in the object relations of these people is obviously of the kind that the milieu of the therapeutic group, which has a "high reality intensity" (Battegay, 1960), is ever necessary to make them stick with their intention to reduce their body weight. That is to say, in their oral expectations and tendencies toward fusion, these individuals may instead become group-dependant. But we should not deplore this result: Only in this manner can their food dependence be relieved.

As these findings show, the large majority of obese people experienced an emotional deficiency in early childhood. They are continually searching for the ideal object they did not receive in the earliest phase of their life. Since in the long run no object can prove to be as ideal as these persons expect it, it is evident that basically good objects may turn into bad ones, as is normally the case in earliest childhood; and thus, as Melanie Klein (1932) explains it, a *splitting* occurs into good and bad objects: A child who finds food on a table judges this piece of furniture to be good, but if the child hits its head on this same table, it becomes a bad object. By excessive food intake, obese persons try to obtain that "good object," but the moment they have swallowed it, it becomes a "bad object," since they cannot effectively become satiated through this object. An insatiable person remains forever insatiated. Learning processes within the family as well as the number and size of the person's fat cells are additional factors determining excessive food intake.

As mentioned above, in a therapeutic group of obese females it became evident that the patients lost weight significantly while participating in the group. At follow-up approximately 2 years later, the weight reduction was no longer significant compared with the beginning of group psychotherapy, though the general trend was still present. The group was experienced by these people as a good object only while it lasted. Obese persons look for momentary pleasure and in this respect are very similar to other addicts. There is no long-lasting satisfaction of their— orally and narcissistically based—hunger for objects. Scarcely have they swallowed an object or fused with it that they become scared of losing the character of the incorporated or fused object. Obese people should, therefore, like other addicts remain integrated in a group as long as possible, in order to have an object at their disposal for continuous incorporation, introjection or fusion.

The treatment of the obese is in itself a very difficult problem because of their tendency toward uncontrolled, addictive food intake. Individual psychotherapy has not led to the expected results. Stunkard (1980) reports, however, positive outcomes of psychoanalytic treatment of obese people. Also, surgical methods like jejunoileal (entero) bypass operations (Bray, 1980) or gastric bypass operations (Halmi, 1980) may, by creating malabsorption (disturbed utilization) or by reducing the stomach volume, lead to a reduction of food absorption or intake—and thus to a weight reduction. But these methods do not represent an effective therapy of the basic emotional disturbances, despite some reports to the contrary (Bray, 1980). The resulting, in part considerable, physical harm is both morphologically and with respect to the digestive process so substantial that the self or the experience of self-esteem in these persons may be damaged even further. This is why psychotherapeutic methods, especially group psychotherapy, should be developed further in these patients. Diet prescriptions and recommendations of changing eating habits or omitting the usual food intake practices or rituals may also have a positive influence. In their helplessness, these emotionally infantile patients usually appreciate receiving diet instructions in the sense of the French word "régime" (cf. "regimen"). The experiences of self-help groups such as "Weight Watchers," which report successful weight reduction among their members with long-term participation, seem to confirm that these people need, on the one hand, permanent support and care through a group as well as, on the other hand, stiff organization ("regimen"). The successes of Ferguson (1975) are to be seen in the same sense. He recommends to his patients a food-intake program on five levels:

- Daily planning
- Establishment of a menu comprising time, place, type and quantity of the foreseen food intake
- Preplanning the food intake in restaurants and at parties
- Preparing daily meals in the morning, in order to reduce the tendency toward eating between meals
- Preplanning the buying of food through exact lists and buying only on a full stomach so that nothing is bought that is not marked on the list.

That computer diets have little chance for success is obvious when the emotional needs of these "hunger" patients are considered.

❖The "Hunger" for Warmth, Stimulation and Fusion in Narcissistically Disturbed People

Human beings who, in their earliest childhood and during further development, do not receive the loving care and warmth, the stimulation—not only tactile, but also visual and acoustic stimulation—as well as the cognitive possibilities necessary to becoming a healthy adult, will always "hunger" for these missed experiences. But also those who were stimulated and cared for excessively in their earliest childhood and who experienced unlimited cognitive possibilities—having been "entertained" constantly—will later on miss what they received immoderately. And there are yet others who during childhood had to adapt constantly to their mother's or their parents' expectations and, in their constant effort to receive their approval, built up an ideal self but neglected to develop their real self (A. Miller, 1979).

> The author recalls a 40-year-old man who worked successfully as a researcher in a scientific institute. He was obviously very much appreciated by his boss. Because of his high abilities, it was planned that he would head a newly created section within the institute. After he had been informed accordingly, he became anxious, agitated, depressed. Over and over again he wondered whether he was capable of coping with this new task. Finally, his panic reached the point that he visited the Basel Psychiatric Outpatient Clinic. He had grown up as an only child, and his father, being a citizen of a foreign country, had been called up for military service. Thus, the family was tended to by the mother. She expected much of her son, and he did his utmost to make her happy. He became the first in his class at school and proved his high intelligence. The mother was proud of him, and slowly she could forget her sorrow for the absent father. She then turned to her son with all her affection. He became her "king," the embodiment of the mastermind, the good one, the beloved one, the best one. He said to himself: "I cannot disappoint her now, I have to replace my father" (who in the meantime had been killed in action). Again and again he felt that he could not afford to fail. In high school he received the best marks and passed the final examination with excellent scores. Also during his studies at the university he proved to be the best of his class and was his "mother's pride and joy." He spent a few years in training abroad and was appreciated everywhere he went. Wherever he studied and worked, he was considered someone who knew his profession. At the age of 25, he married a very unselfish, devoted and competent woman.

The patient's mother eventually managed to accept her daughter-in-law, although she became depressive after the "loss" (marriage) of her son, as she was emotionally unable to work through the separation. In the course of his work, the patient decided to take a further examination. He prepared himself conscientiously. But on the day of the examination, he "lost his nerves." There was a block, he was unable to remember anything, a lump came into his throat, his mouth dried up, and he failed the examination. He never forgave himself for having failed. In the meantime, three children were born. He saw his career as over. Nevertheless, he continued to take on higher and higher professional positions and became internationally renowned. He worked very hard and diligently in order to keep up his self-confidence. But upon being foreseen for a new position, he was gripped by panic that he would no longer be able to satisfy his superiors. Previously, he had enjoyed having the responsibility for a department; now, he would have had to learn a great deal for the foreseen new work, something he was not totally up to, and he was unable to forgive himself for this. He felt worse and worse and was unable to relax during vacation. He started to have attacks of profuse perspiration. At work, he behaved as if everything was fine; but in fact he was scarcely able to carry out his duties. He could no longer concentrate; worries and doubts began to eat at him; he went from one doctor to the next, but they were unable to help him. Finally, he had to take over the newly created department. He experienced his new work as a never-ending examination and was convinced that everybody was watching him. He continually looked for confirmation, yet no amount of encouragement was sufficient. He wanted to master his work in the new department from the very beginning. This expectation turned out to be unrealistic. He became hesitant and insecure, but insisted on carrying on to the end. A week later he collapsed at his desk. He felt depressed, finished, marked by fate. From the next day on he was incapable of going to work. At home he stayed in bed, but relaxation made everything even worse. Day and night his relatives tried to calm him down, but everything was in vain. Any reassurance, even repeated constantly, did not help. The panic fear of failure was immense. He spent three weeks in a small private hospital where, however, no significant progress was attained. Back at work, he still felt weak, and he was especially afraid of no longer being needed. And he was still depressive. No amount of recognition, no amount of encouragement was of any use. He had to enter a psychiatric inpatient department where he was treated with psychopharmaceutics and supportive psychotherapy. There, in the emotionally warm atmosphere, he was able to recover. When he started his work again, he still had a craving for praise and was anxious that his colleagues and superiors would not think well of him. Psychotherapy therefore was continued intensively on a combined psychoanalytic-cognitive basis, in the sense of building up a consistent self, sound self-esteem, and showing him how much he had gotten used to seeing himself and the world through his mother's eyes—who viewed him as being exceptionally capable, inexhaustible and able to accomplish *everything*. He had to realize how much he too tended to have excessive expectations of himself—expectations he was able to fulfill only as long as his work and his private life continued along well-trodden paths. But whenever he was to take on a new task, he had to pass his own "exams"—and he had already failed one exam when his high expectations caused his panic to be intensified to such an extent that it resulted in complete failure.

The hunger for a fusion with an idealized self-object—in this case the man's mother, but also his wife, colleagues and superiors at work—revealed that because of his ideal self, he had no consistent real self and thus only little narcissistic libido, attention or information at his disposal to invest his basically strong ego. He always had to be sure that others agreed with him in their fantasy—and even then he did not feel satisfied. He was in fact "sick from hunger," not so much in an oral sense, but with respect to his need to experience a constant reinforcement of his damaged narcissism. To stuff this "narcissistic hole" (Ammon, 1974) was, of course, not feasible, as the early spoiling on the part of his mother had led to insatiability.

Those who are constantly looking for confirmation, who need constant praise and applause—this can also often be seen in politicians—have a weak self-esteem. Their insatiable "hunger" for reinforcement shows that, in fact, they do not dominate the field—on the contrary, they are completely dependent on their surroundings.

The narcissism of these people's needs is always such that they are insatiable and have an addictive character. Later we shall go into this in greater detail.

For now I would like to mention that narcissistic hunger always embraces the danger of incorporating so much and taking possession of so much that the people concerned may actually die because of the appropriated objects. The author's maternal grandmother used to say: "You have to know when you've had enough." She was a well-balanced, albeit serious-minded, upright person, who, it seemed to me, never had to ponder much over what was right or wrong. Obviously, her life experience had taught her that one can lead a quiet and well-balanced life only by accepting one's boundaries and the limitations of one's activities.

As Margaret Mahler (1968) observed, certain people have not—from earliest childhood on—had the possibility of experiencing the warmth, stimulation and Gestalt-configurations offered them. Their mothers have greater problems producing a smile on their face, even as small babies. Such a congenital or very early deficit may also manifest itself by the baby not being able to signal that it would like to receive more attention.

In the research of D. Stern and B. Beebe (1977) with homozygotic twins videotaped in their second week of life together with their mothers, it turned out, among other things, that the mother paid considerably less attention to one child than to the other. The baby receiving more attention had more opportunity to imitate the mother's mouth movements and therefore appeared to be more active. In these videotapes, it was also observed that the baby was able to see the mother's mouth movements already in the second week of life. This proved that focused sight does not arise together with the "three-month smile" observed in babies, but in fact very much earlier. These investigations concern our subject of hunger inasmuch as we have to ask ourselves *why* the mother paid more attention to one twin and less to the other. One may speculate that, for some unknown reason, one baby was more able to "motivate" the mother's attention than the twin.

Since the ego is not completely developed immediately after birth, but probably only genetically determined ego cores (Hartmann, 1964) exist, one cannot ascribe the better ability to send the mother signals to the baby's ego strength. Yet certain babies are better able to mobilize other people, especially the mother, to give them stimuli from the very beginning. One could, therefore, formulate it rather grotesquely that everyone determines his or her own education. In this sense, those children remain "hunger-sick" who were not sufficiently able to gather the interest of their surroundings, primarily the mother. Of course, there are also those who, through no predisposition, did not receive enough cognitive stimulation, emotional warmth and Gestalt-offers, and are subsequently disturbed in their experience of self-value: These are people with narcissistic neuroses (narcissistic personality disorders). Then there are also the borderline personalities described by Kernberg (1975/1981/1984), Rohde-Dachser (1982) and others, who, as already described, were since birth—mainly because of their genetically determined weakness—neither sufficiently able to experience the love and cognitive stimulation offered, nor capable of gaining the interest of the mother or any other important person: These individuals have a weak ego with a tendency toward fragmentation—together with a rigid defense meant to help them to prevent the menacing breakthrough of unconscious impulses—who despite, or perhaps because of, their rigid defense tend to experience uncontrolled breakthroughs. Also, they often tend to confuse their inner world with outside reality. Their view of objects results in their splitting them into "good" and "bad" ones (Melanie Klein, 1932), with "good" objects being those with which they can temporarily fuse in their fantasy, whereas the "bad" ones do not allow such a relationship—or on the contrary allow such a strong fusion that these people feel afraid of losing their ego boundaries and thus their ego. Borderline personalities, being primarily disturbed in their capacity to communicate, are hardly able to build up a mature object relationship. For the most part, as mentioned, they tend to take up a fusionary contact with others and to experience the object primarily as "good"; yet when this fusionary relationship is no longer possible or becomes too intensive, they secondarily experience the same object as "bad." As much as these individuals may desire social contacts, they remain hungry.

A 35-year-old illegitimately born woman had a mother who, on the one hand, had no moral principles and numerous male acquaintances, also during her marriage, but, on the other hand, established very strong rules for her daughter in this respect. She grew up in an emotionally extremely poor environment. When the patient was 2 years old, the mother married. The patient did not experience any love at all, and after her half-brother was killed in an accident—she was 6 years old at the time—she was mistreated. From her ninth year on, her stepfather sexually abused her. At the age of 11 she had her first period. The intimate relations with her stepfather lasted until she was 13. The girl was then put into a religious boarding school where she was abused by lesbians. She escaped and went home where the abuse continued. In her 19th year, in her immense hunger for a human relationship, she became attached to a man, became pregnant and gave birth to a girl, but felt herself put under pressure by the authorities to give up the child for adoption. Although she dearly wanted to keep the baby, she gave in. At 24, she married a mechanic, 4 years her senior, who was divorced from his first wife. Since he had to pay support for two children, he had to work very hard. Because of her fear of becoming pregnant again—the pill did not agree with her—it often came to tensions between them during the first years of marriage. She thought she was a burden to her husband and agreed to a divorce. At age 32, she was alone again. She attempted suicide several times, was repeatedly put into a psychiatric hospital and received outpatient psychiatric treatment. From her life history it was also known that, for no apparent organic reason, she underwent a hysterectomy at the age of 25 since she was suffering from abdominal cramps. At 28, a fibrositis syndrome began to appear. Today, the patient is dependent on social welfare, having failed to apply for a disability pension in due time.

As this patient's life story shows, she was, probably also because of a genetic disposition, unable to obtain sufficient attention and stimulation; her mother's deviant character already shows a certain familial component in this respect. In addition, there is the horrible and psychotraumatic milieu. The patient was scarcely able to develop a self and an object representation. She became anxious when anything was demanded of her. Somehow she expected that the objects she met were "good" to her, but they all proved to be "bad." Even now she sees the world according to her own inner world. She cannot deal with reality, fails to, or is unable to, defend her position in the world. Occasionally, she shows impulse breakthroughs in form of suicide attempts. If she encounters a psychotherapist or a physician who shows understanding, she enters into a fusion with them in her fantasy. If she feels temporarily misunderstood, she is unable to keep up a relationship and switches therapists. As she herself mentioned, her work was her escape from the world. She apparently built up a rigid defense against her drives and against threats from the outside world, though not always with success. The moment the fibrositis syndrome appeared, she was no longer able to continue her work: Her defense system collapsed. That was one reason why she undertook the suicidal acts.

The patient suffers from a hunger disease because she cannot get her human environment to show enough interest in her, and because she let herself be included too much in the plans of others and thereby obtained too little for herself. In the author's experience, such a patient can be helped only by being placed in a therapeutic group of similarly afflicted people working with an experienced therapist. In this way, she can be integrated into a milieu in which she can once again experience emotional participation to the point of being able to perceive it. The intensity of the group interactions will help her to better understand the dynamics of social reality.

❖Hunger in Depressives and Addicts

In all addictions there is an insatiable hunger for new objects to fill an inner emptiness—the gap between will and ability, between wish and reality, between illusion and truth, between appearance and existence. People who have only an insufficient self or an insufficient feeling of self-esteem, be it genetically determined or from experiences of real deficiency in early childhood, tend to desire fusion with objects in order to experience a reinforcement of their selves. The "narcissistic hole" (Ammon, 1974) must be filled with humans or objects the people concerned take or would like to take possession of or would like to swallow. We have often observed in individuals who tend to steal during depressive phases that their pathological tendency is the result of the unconscious desire to take possession of objects in order to reinforce their selves. The stolen objects are meant to give these people a strength they otherwise cannot attain. Often, such people have an insatiable and unsurmountable desire to take possession of objects without the true intention of enriching themselves materially. They may store the objects in the basement or somewhere in their apartment without any use for them. This type of hoarding seems to serve unconsciously to let them feel reinforced.

A 56-year-old woman was sent to the Basel Outpatient Department from criminal court for examination. She had been caught in a department store stealing blouses, handbags and a cardigan. The examining officer who questioned her on the thefts noticed she was depressive and otherwise psychologically conspicuous. Thus, a psychiatric opinion was requested.

She was born as the daughter of a high state employee of a foreign country. The father decided not to marry her mother. The patient knew him only from a photograph, though she did get to know him personally when she was 19. The mother was 24 years old when she gave birth to the daughter. She was an industry worker, good-natured and diligent. The patient spent the first years of her life at the home of her father's parents abroad—the father obviously had only little contact with his parents. She has good memories of the time with her paternal grandparents. When she was 6, the mother met a man and married him a year later. It seems that her stepfather was jealous of the grandparents. This was apparently the reason why the mother took the child back home after getting married. During the day she was placed in foster families where she had a very hard time. She was good in school. The patient was antagonistic toward her stepfather: She apparently experienced in him only refusal, negative criticism and physical beatings. At 16, she had her first period. She had not been informed by her mother about sexuality—at home they never spoke about "those things." At the age of 19, she received a letter from her father and subsequently met with him. The meeting was a big disappointment, since her father spoke ill of the mother. In the same year she began work as a saleswoman. A year later she started to work as an office worker in the publicity department of a big company, where she stayed for 8 years. At the beginning, she handed over her entire salary at home, but after 5 years she left home and took a rented room, since the tension between her and her stepfather had reached a level that she was unable to continue to live there. At 29, she became engaged to a academic 15 years her elder. During the next 8 years she was attached to him. She experienced this relationship as very harmonious in every respect. But 6 months before the planned marriage, her fiancé abandoned her. She tried to commit suicide with painkillers. Consequently, she changed her job and worked as a secretary for 11 years. In order to overcome the disappointment with her fiancé, she concentrated entirely on her work. In those years she realized for the first time that she loved to buy a lot of clothes; she had the impression that she was trying to prove something to herself. In the same year she started her new work, her mother died from intestinal cancer. Her death affected the patient enormously. Since then she suffered from gastrointestinal disturbances as well as from migraine and hypertension. During a walk one Sunday at the age of 45, she met a company clerk who was 3 years younger than herself. They got married 2 years later. At the beginning, the marriage was satisfactory. With time, however, they drifted apart. They slept in separate bedrooms, and soon they even ate separately. One year later, at the request of her husband, the patient stopped working for a while. Three years later, at the age of 50, she entered menopause. She went to see a gynaecologist because of hot and cold spells. Her tendency to buy clothes and bags reached an extreme. Soon she began to work again as a secretary. The differences with her husband became ever greater, and he started to beat her. With her salary she bought clothes and started to fill up the closets and wardrobes of the whole house. At age 56, after an argument with her husband, she stole clothes in two department stores.

In the interviews it became clear that this patient had an immense and insatiable need for human warmth and love, but that she was constantly frustrated because external reality was unable to offer her what she desired. She experienced herself as alone in the world, felt lonesome and abandoned. The patient looked older than she actually was and gave the impression of being a desperate depressive. She reported how she had glorified her father in the photo and how disappointed she had been when she met him later on. Apparently she suffered a lot in the foster families she had to stay with during the day after having moved into her mother's home. She also suffered from being separated from her grandparents who had brought her up in her earliest childhood. She was helpless in the marital situation, receiving from her husband neither warmth nor love. The biggest disappointment for her was the failure of her partnership with the older academic. The patient received a narcissistic injury she was unable to overcome. She said she felt very depressive, oppressed, desperate and tense before her thefts. Why she had stolen was unclear to her, but after the thefts she apparently felt somehow relieved. She accepted the risk of getting into trouble with the police since in this way she was at least able to experience a human encounter.

Her stealing clothes obviously had the unconscious function of compensating her with these objects. She was trying to strengthen herself narcissistically at a moment at which she particularly felt her loneliness. In her earliest childhood she had scarcely experienced the sheltered home that is necessary to building up a healthy self-esteem. The collapse of the friendship with her older academic friend led to a narcissistic injury that revived her needs, and her marriage injured her continuously, so that the described theft occurred after only a minor additional burden.

In our statement for the court we declared this depressive woman to be not responsible for her actions, since the motives for the thefts were unconscious to her, and in the past she had not been exposed to such illegal impulses. Earlier she had satisfied her needs and strengthened her self legally, by buying a lot of clothes. In a severely depressive condition, after an argument with her husband, her desire had become so abrupt and overwhelming that she stole the clothes without further thought.

The motives behind the thefts are not consciously apparent to such depressives. They are unable to explain their acts. When threatened with the loss of contact to an object or objects, they apparently try to compensate for this danger by taking possession of other ones. Unconscious tendencies of fusion with and taking possession of objects play a role here. Sabine Keller (1981a, b) has compared this depressive type of theft with the purely neurotic one in which various neurotic drive disturbances manifest themselves. Another kind of theft is found in kleptomania, which proves to be a sexual drive substitute. In again another type of theft, that committed by fetishists, the stolen symbolic objects unconsciously have, pars pro toto, a sexual significance. We therefore recognize four different types of theft without the conscious purpose of personal enrichment: 1) depressive, 2) neurotic, 3) kleptomaniac, 4) fetishistic.

Arthur Kielholz (1920) observed that there are criminal acts for which no or nearly no motive can be found. These acts do not fit the personality of the perpetrator, and the circumstances are strange. These "symbolic thefts," as Kielholz called them, are similar to the symbolic actions of obsessive-compulsive neurotics, but also to those faulty actions mentioned by Sigmund Freud in his *Psychopathology of Everyday Life* (1960) as expressing unconscious symbolic intentions. An addictive character is present, however, above all in thefts by depressives, since in these individuals taking possession of something leads to a reduction of tension and relief only for a short time. Soon afterwards, a similar act must be done to tranquillize the "hunger" of these people in their damaged self—to fill up their narcissistic emptiness. When speaking here of a tendency in depressives toward addictively taking possession of things we are also inclined to wonder whether all passionate collectors of whatever items suffer more or less unconsciously from such a hunger disease. Do large art collections protect their weak self? It is well known how much social prestige goes along with such a collection. Those concerned may, for that reason alone, feel more self-confident, receiving more attention from others and basking or mirroring themselves in their applause. But, as already mentioned, also those who eat insatiably and to no end desire basically to obtain the love they did not receive in their early childhood and afterwards were not able to experience. To these people the addictive incorporation and taking possession of objects means taking and incorporating objects that otherwise might be withheld from them.

Sigmund Freud (1916) and Karl Abraham (1924) have spoken of the tendency of the endogenous (major) depressives to incorporate both the beloved and simultaneously abhorred object, and to treat the ego as if it were this object. Freud mentioned in this context the reversal of the aggression toward the ego. Accordingly, in depressives we see the tendency to expect total attention from close persons of reference. But since the attention can never be as much as they desire, aggressions arise that are rarely directed toward the actual object, but rather toward the ego.

Elsewhere the author has argued (1977) that there is no narcissistic energy (libido, attention, information) left in depressives to invest the ego and the objects, and that aggressive impulses are therefore not directed only onto objects, but also onto the ego, which is equally experienced as estranged. This statement corresponds to one aspect of the explanation of the dynamics of depressives. Another aspect is certainly that mentioned by Freud and Abraham, both of whom in fact recognized in depressives very early on the tendency toward fusion. In these individuals object and subject are not strictly separated. They tend to "eat up" the object in an addictive manner. Fenichel (1946) spoke in this context of "love addicts."

Those who treat or deal with depressives know that the people in question demand so much attention that the work is not only challenging but often also exhausting. Sometimes when the depressive is recovering, the previously healthy partner starts to become depressive. It is interesting to note that the partners of depressives normally stand up for the patients and look after them unselfishly—contrary to the relatives of schizophrenics, who often experience the patients as so different that they leave them. The families of depressives are more constant than those of schizophrenics. During a study at the Basel Psychiatric Outpatient Clinic this fact was also determined quantitatively (Battegay et al., 1972).

It has repeatedly been noticed that adolescent drug dependents are in fact not asocial, as the public would like to have it, but on the contrary demand *too much* of the social order: In their earliest childhood they were mostly cared for insufficiently or were unable to experience the love shown toward them—and were thus bound to be disappointed. In some cases they were overprotected and secondarily experienced the world as frustrating. Unconsciously, they then have the expectation that their human environment should understand and accept them unconditionally, whatever they do. These youngsters implicitly expect those responsible in society to keep things going, while they for themselves—addictively—require continuous love and understanding.

The manifestation of discontent and protest by adolescents throughout the world today may be conditioned by their entertainment of high expectations toward the "winners" and their subsequent disappointment because those responsible are not ready to give them, on the one hand, the attention demanded nor, on the other hand, the external autonomy that, in their opinion, would make them happy. These young people—hungry for emotions and life—through their protest marches, through their outrage, hope to encounter the representatives of a society who up till now have withdrawn from them; with their parents or substitutes they have never been able to experience the struggle of opinions which they would have needed, and which would have helped them to develop autonomy. Often the so-called healthy adults are still so unsatiated in their own hunger for life that they not only desire ever greater successes in their profession, but also supply themselves with an increasing number of stimuli in their leisure time. They have little time and energy left for the education of their children. In our affluent society, often the children have, as a replacement for love, been infinitely spoiled materially, but have never received the loving attention that alone would enable the encounter they so much need in order to recognize their fellow human beings as such.

The time of those adolescents and young adults who wished to destroy the old authoritarian structures during the so-called "1968 revolution" has long passed. The schools and universities have been restructured in an authoritarian manner, and many young people have since felt resigned. They are all too willing to accept the imposed order, though often showing little motivation for their studies or apprenticeship. When the most disadvantaged ones demonstrate in the street, one may presume it is a desperate outcry from those who have experienced only meager human relationships, and who have great difficulties finding their place in our modern computer society.

Young people who do not understand the possibilities of modern electronic data processing or who are little motivated to pursue them will have the feeling of being disadvantaged and of being able to assume only auxiliary functions in society. It is no longer the question of people having enough financial means to make a bare living, since the state's unemployment payments and other social services generally secure one's living. What worries these young people—and a lot of adults—is the fact that they don't feel useful anymore. They have an immense hunger for a significant activity, but are left to themselves and constantly reminded that society drops enough crumbs from the table so that they can feed themselves. In their hopelessness and resignation they feel threatened and long for work and recognition. They are not interested in living a life of contemplation; they would not even be able to do that since it would be meaningless to them. Whereas Karl Marx (1872) envisaged social classes defined particularly through material aspects, we think that today a new classification is arising: One part of society will actively participate in the computer achievements, some will have only auxiliary functions, and some will even not have the opportunity to work. The essential point of these three classes is no longer one's material income—which will, to a certain extent, be secured for everybody—but the feeling and the knowledge of being useful for something, or occupying a subordinate function or having no function at all in society. Not being able to contribute productively and resolutely to a goal and the accomplishment of a task is depressing. Taking drugs may partly reflect the despair arising from the external situation, but partly also the wish to overcome narcissistic emptiness. The "high" experienced after drug intake as well as the incorporation of or the taking possession of an object cause those concerned to get the feeling that they have done something to reinforce their self-esteem, although the narcissistic reinforcement soon proves to be illusory, since it is only transient and requires continuous repetition.

A 22-year-old man whose parents divorced early grew up as an only child with his mother and his stepfather. His mother, a waitress, came from another country and was apparently never able to become accustomed to her new surroundings. She needed psychiatric outpatient treatment. The patient has no contact to a brother from the same marriage. Up to the age of 10 the patient bit his nails, had problems at school, and often did not attend classes. He was then put into a home for two years where he did not complete his apprenticeship as vintager. During his basic military training he came down with hepatitis. At age 22 he entered a hospital because of his heroin dependence. It was striking that he had little contact with the other patients. He tended to react obstinately after experiencing frustrations, but at the same time made unrealistic and exaggerated plans for his future. His self-esteem was unstable. During the psychotherapeutic sessions it emerged that he had not had enough love and attention from his mother during childhood and needed a more constant milieu. He had lived alternately with his parents and in a children's home. His mother was unable to give him a feeling of security, and the stepfather tended to fulfill his every wish but did not give him any guiding principles. Eventually, this second marriage of his mother also ended in divorce. The patient decided to stay with his stepfather. Nevertheless (or perhaps for that very reason), he felt torn between his mother and his stepfather. His heroin abuse started after he came down with hepatitis. Before he had consumed marijuana and occasionally LSD. The patient realized himself that he tended to live in a fusionary relationship with his stepfather. He was not able to become independent, did not find a suitable job and suffered greatly from this. Tempted by the respective milieu, he began taking drugs. They were unconsciously meant to help him to establish his own world and to reinforce his self-esteem. When on drugs, no one could reach him, and he had no desire to merge completely with his stepfather. During his drug ecstasy he was also able to live out his high-flying plans—without being reminded by reality that he had scarcely developed his own identity.

Alcohol dependents too have the tendency to try to incorporate otherwise unreachable objects. A Swiss vernacular term is to drink a "Schoppe" (baby bottle) or to "mämmele" (call for one's mother). These phrases indicate that the—oral—incorporation, and certainly also the narcissistic reinforcement of imbibing this type of "mother's milk," contributes to their drinking habits. Further reflective of their hunger disease are the gastric and duodenal ulcers often found in the life history of alcohol dependents before they began to drink (Labhardt, 1964). Both alcohol dependence and the ulcers are symptoms of the underlying basic hunger disease.

We had to care for a 41-year-old man from Italy. He was born as the second of four children and grew up in a large farmer's family that was "governed" by the grandfather in a patriarchal way. The father, who was severe and showed little understanding, died at the age of 39 of tuberculosis. At the time of her son's consultations in our outpatient clinic, the mother was still living in her native country. During the patient's childhood, she had little time for her children, since she worked in a factory. The patient's grandmother and his aunt offered a certain substitute. During his childhood, the patient experienced the grandfather and his father's brothers as threatening, much like his own father. As a child, he was physically weak, so that his family could not resort to him for agricultural labor. He was an anxious, self-absorbed child who had little contact to other children. His father's death hit him at the age of 9. Together with one of his sisters he had to leave the large family to live with the family of one of their uncles for 2 years. There, he was apparently beaten repeatedly. Later on he was able to return to his own family. He attended school up to the age of 14, but because of test anxiety was not able to finish his education. And that he did not feel attracted to girls, but rather to boys made him even more fearful and uncommunicative, since he was unable to talk things over with anyone. After finishing school, he had to work hard in his profession as a salesman. He lived with his mother and sisters and felt completely misunderstood. He could talk with no one about his homosexual tendencies. Later he worked for a liquor company. During this time he started to drink. As he saw it, only then was he able to "overcome" his social difficulties and his homophile tendencies. In Switzerland he hoped to find the security he needed and moved there in 1961. First, he worked as a waiter and then, after taking courses, as a hairdresser. Finally, he found a friend and lived with him for 6 years. In this relationship he found the security he had been unable to experience earlier. After a triangular relationship had developed, the patient suffered a lot and consequently separated from his friend. Soon a gastric ulcer developed, and he had to be operated on. During this time he began drinking again excessively and had to be hospitalized in a psychiatric hospital for a week. There he was put on disulfirame (Antatus) and remained under the control of a social worker. He was, however, unable to continue his work regularly. He then further lost the control over his alcohol consumption and had to be supported financially by his mother. His former friend also tried to help him, but the patient constantly felt disappointed by him, since this man refused to renew their sexual relationship. His timidity, his contact problems, his absence of self-confidence rendered any new relationship impossible. At home in his apartment he was tortured by anxiety. Finally, there was nothing else to do but to start again inpatient treatment in a hospital.

This patient was "brought up" as a child, but enjoyed no heartfelt nurturing. Especially from his father and grandfather he came to know masculinity as something threatening, and he had a lifelong desire for the fatherly nearness as well as motherly warmth that would have allowed him to develop a consistent self. His homosexual tendencies as well as his inclination to drink alcohol excessively served to fill up his "narcissistic hole" and to strengthen his self-esteem. His "hunger" for other men and his "thirst" for alcohol showed that he was basically fixated on a narcissistic-oral level of development, and that he tried to take possession of or to fuse with the objects that had been withheld from him earlier.

As we have seen, in depressives as in addicts, hunger can drive people so far that they incorporate and take possession of objects uncritically and scarcely notice that these processes have taken place. Yet this is not astonishing: Whoever tries to appropriate objects totally, either in an oral-incorporative or in a narcissistic-fusionary manner, tends to deny the independence of these objects and at the same time to lose sight of their actual value. The French saying *tout embrasser c'est tout perdre* ("To embrace it is to lose it") expresses this insight perfectly. To embrace or to take total possession of an object or even the entire object world means remaining without means of communication since one is then unable to perceive the objects as such. It is not by chance that depressives and addicts show this tendency: Both are disturbed, damaged in their self-esteem. Their ability to narcissistically invest their ego, their id, their superego, their body and the objects is damaged. Whether we express ourselves energetically (instinct theory) or according to the theory of cognition or according to information theory; whether we say they have too little narcissistic libido at their disposal or cannot summon enough narcissistic attention or cannot transfer enough narcissistic information (e.g., to their ego)—we always mean that the respective individuals have a deficiency, partially or totally, in their selves and thus in their self-image and self-esteem. Depressives and addicts suffer severely from this narcissistic deficiency. Contrary to those who suffer exclusively from a narcissistic personality disorder (narcissistic neurosis) without any substantial accompanying depression and without any tendency toward addiction, depressives or addicts tend to fuse totally with, to be dependent on, and to affix themselves to objects.

When these people commit a theft, one has to take into account that they often cannot bear their inner emptiness and have the overwhelming desire to take possession of an object in order to calm themselves down. They are no doubt able to gain insight into the wrongness of their action, but they are rarely or even not at all able to act according to this insight, since they experience the "narcissistic hole," the deficiency in their self, as unbearable. Thus, the people concerned are more or less not legally responsible for the offenses they are accused of. The hunger of depressives and addicts, however, can never be satiated.

> The author recalls an elderly, extremely depressive woman who piled up stolen goods in her cellar. She had absolutely no use for them, nearly forgot their presence in fact and felt as unhappy as before. She may have felt a short relief while stealing an object, but her habitual unhappy state soon overcame her.

In addicts of all kinds—and not only in drug dependents, but also in people addicted to collecting things or addicted to eating things—the pleasure after having incorporated an object is for the most part very short-lived. In German there is the saying "I could eat myself to death," which means that for someone addicted to food intake the limit is reached only when they die of overeating. Other popular sayings are also known, such as: "He (or she) can never get enough." This points to the insatiability of the individuals concerned. We've also seen people who are addicted to approval, whereby it is commonly known that those who want to be liked by everyone have hidden problems. In our context, we recognize this problem as the need for narcissistic fusion, confirmation and mirroring.

The insatiability of addicts for emotional approval can also be observed in group psychotherapy with them. The participants of such groups become dependent on the collective, so that group treatment can not be terminated at will.

From 1957 to 1967, the author led a group of 7 to 9 medicament-dependent, middle-aged women in the Basel University Psychiatric Inpatient Department. There, we observed that all patients, with the exception of one, relapsed after leaving the group and the hospital for an outpatient facility. This too proves that addicts generally—and not only the obese—constantly need an object that will allow them to overcome their narcissistic deficiency and to compensate their hunger. This means that "food addicts" as well as all other addicts cannot simply renounce the objects they addictively consume, but rather are in need of a substitute. Through participation in group therapy, addicts tend to become group-dependent. One could regret that these persons cannot develop complete autonomy. One can, however, reply that obese people ("food addicts") as well as drug dependents often *never* reach full autonomy. If not exploited ideologically or politically, group dependence would certainly be less harmful than obesity or any other dependence. Later in old age, when they have less narcissistic needs, they may perhaps be able to live without this constant support by a group of likewise affected persons, that is, only when their narcissistic hunger has become less intensive are they able to find their way without the support of a group. Ciompi and Eisert (1971) have stated that former drug dependents (albeit a relatively smaller than average number ever reach older age, since they have a higher than average morbidity and mortality rate) are in old age often able to lead a quiet and settled life without resorting to the previously abused substances.

❖The Insatiable, Destructive Tendency Toward Total Fusion with an Object and Its Subsequent Destruction

As I have mentioned elsewhere (Battegay, 1981), people whose experience of self-esteem and conceptions of other human beings are severely disturbed—expressed in psychoanalytic language, they are disturbed in their self- and object representation—often expect that those they encounter or work with should integrate themselves more or less completely into their own fantasy world. Such people were either genetically (because of a proneness to ego fragmentation) unable to motivate their mothers to give them enough love and attention, or they were originally genetically normal but, because of neglect or overprotection or growing up having to fulfill mother's and father's expectations to be an ideal child, had no opportunity to build up a solid self-representation and object representation corresponding to outside reality (Mahler, 1968). Hartmann (1964) has pointed out that the ego usually has full potentials at its disposal to allow the social integration of the individual who is adapted (but not over-adapted) to reality and does not expect that others should be subordinate. Yet, as mentioned, an individual can, for genetic or environmental reasons, be hindered in ego development. Kohut (1971/1977) and O. F. Kernberg (1975/1981/1984) have described disorders resulting from deficiencies of emotional warmth and stimulation in earliest childhood, or from insufficient sensitivity for emotional attention from a genetic predisposition: These are the *narcissistic personality disorders* (narcissistic neuroses), which originate mostly in one's early life history; and the *borderline personality disorders*, which are mainly determined genetically, though they also result from insufficient experiences of attention or overprotection or an incapacity to feel and register maternal warmth.

In patients with narcissistic personality and borderline personality disorders, the tendency may be found to compensate their deficient self: They show fantasies of grandeur, the wish to fuse in their fantasy with idealized objects as well as a tendency toward mirror relations or transferences (Battegay, 1977). Accordingly, they tend to see objects as they need them for inner reasons. The fantasies of grandeur help them to consider the object as an attribute of themselves. Other human beings are there to reflect the feelings of the narcissistically disturbed individuals—not their own emotions. Especially borderline patients tend toward projective identification and, as Melanie Klein (1932), Kernberg (1975/1981/1984) and others have observed, tend to split objects according to archaic experience into good or bad ones: An object that makes fusion possible is thus a good one; but it becomes a bad object if it recognizes that it would lose its independence through fusion and stops the previous attitude. Borderline patients, with their fusion tendencies and—on this basis—projective identifications, then see the aggressive parts of their own ego in the object. Thus, an object, used or misused in this way, refuses to adapt to the narcissistic demands of such an individual, and uncontrolled outbreaks of aggression result, as described by Kohut (1971/1977) and Kernberg (1975/1981). Someone with such a tendency toward fusion will become even more angry upon discovering his or her dependence on objects. Mende (1967) found that patients who have committed sudden homicidal acts show similar dynamics.

Erich Fromm (1973) emphasizes that injured narcissism is one of the most important sources of defensive aggression. The author can only partly agree with this statement. If Fromm wishes to differentiate between defensive (benign) aggression and destructive (malign) aggression, then certainly aggression arising from injured narcissism would be the destructive one. Fromm speaks of *necrophilia*, i.e., the passion to change something living into something nonliving, to destroy for the purpose of destruction: The only interest present is purely mechanical. In Fromm's view, this is the desire to dismember living connections. He fails to bring this tendency into connection with narcissistic rage, the narcissistic need for revenge, the tendency to let others suffer for one's own narcissistic deficiency and injury. He describes the necrophilic character by saying that such an individual experiences only the past, but neither the present nor the future, as totally real. What is past—what is *dead*—dominates this person's life: institutions, laws, property, traditions, possessions. In short, objects dominate humans, possession dominates existence, the dead dominate the living. As Fromm said, in the personal philosophical and political thinking of the necrophilic, the past is holy, nothing new is of value, a drastic change is a crime against the "natural order." Fromm describes here essen-

70

tially individuals who, in their earliest childhood, did not experience a warm and stimulating experience of objects and sufficient Gestalt-cognitions, and who were never able to develop warm feelings toward their mother—be it because they were genetically unable to experience the mother's feelings, because their mother was a cold individual, because in early childhood they always had to adapt to the expectations of their parents, or because the conditions of a broken home were traumatizing. Fromm (1973) speaks of human beings who are not able to accept reality, but he sees other reasons for this than the author has presented in this volume: Fromm thinks that an anal-sadistic tendency in these individuals lies at the basis of their difficulties. He maintains that necrophilia can be defined as the malign form of the anal character.

It is, however, our experience, which we would like to prove with some examples, that these individuals do not resemble anal characters, who simply desire to possess objects to enrich themselves and do not like to experience changes; rather, they are people who do not experience the objects as something separate from themselves. In their fantasy they do not really possess the objects, but undergo a fusion with them, through which the objects then no longer exist as such. If an object becomes active and is recognized as such because it does not behave as in the fusion fantasies of the narcissistically disturbed individuals with their narcissistic personality disorders or especially borderline personality disorders, then there are two possibilities: They feel narcissistically injured or menaced by the object or even—at least temporarily—persecuted by it; or they destroy the object.

These severe narcissistic personality disorders and borderline personality disorders with narcissistic disturbances play a major role especially in forensic psychiatry. When preparing a psychiatric report for the courts on such people who have threatened someone, one should keep in mind that they can in fact be quite dangerous to those with whom they have undergone a fusion in their fantasy—especially when their victims have suddenly laid claim to their independence. If a homicide has already been committed, it is virtually impossible to say that such a person would never kill an object again if the same tendencies toward fusion are still present or if a fusion has been dissolved.

A 23-year-old man grew up under unfavorable family conditions, the son of a father who refused to work and of an affectively reserved mother who rejected her children. At the age of 4 he was put in an orphanage. He showed prolonged thumbsucking, bedwetting until he entered school, nailbiting and a disturbed language development with stuttering. Despite his average intelligence he had great difficulties in learning. Often he did not go to school or ran from the classroom. Occasionally, he committed small thefts. On the other hand, he could also be very nice, adapting himself in a way so that at first his petty crimes were not taken seriously. At age 15, his first girlfriend died. Thereafter, he suffered an epileptic seizure, though the diagnosis of epilepsy was verified only 6 years later. He did not stay long at his jobs, since he had no discipline and committed thefts. Nor could he live for long anywhere after leaving the orphanage, for he did not respond to offers of help. While at military school at age 20, he did not return from leave and was prosecuted. Soon afterwards he stole a large amount of money from the doctor treating him, a neurologist. More and more this man lost complete sight of law and order and soon committed more major thefts. A new psychiatric opinion was requested by court because at age 23 he had helped his half-brother to kill his fiancée, a woman of 32 years. He held the woman's legs while his half-brother strangled her. In the examinations for the opinion, this man behaved so aggressively and imperiously that he was not able to submit to questioning. In the last session, he said that in prison (where he now was at his own request, having begun his term earlier than foreseen) he had gotten to know a man named Daniel who was approximately 31 years old. Through him, he declared, for the first time in his life he had experienced a love that had given him strength. They now had, he said, a sexual relationship and were faithful to each other. Were one of them to neglect this fidelity, he would be killed by the other. He also declared that if he were discharged from prison earlier than his friend, he would kill a woman, and his friend would do the same if discharged earlier. He was shown the danger of such fantasies, but he kept saying that he knows only one method of coexistence, that of a total unity with his friend. All other solutions, he said, would cause him either to kill a woman or to beat her to a pulp. When the author tried to point out that he could never expect such a total unity with another human being, he seemed to understand, but he insisted that his present friend had given him an absolute strength. During the entire examination this man wore a leather jacket given him as a present by his friend, and he refused to take it off when requested to do so.

Among the applied psychological tests, the German version of the *Wechsler Intelligence Test for Adults* (HAWIE) resulted in an intelligence quotient of 96 (verbal part: 96, performance part: 97). In the attention-stress test, the patient worked extremely slowly, though with good quality. In the *Benton Test* there was no decrease in achievement. Accordingly, an organic brain disorder could be excluded. In the color pyramid test it became obvious that he had difficulties mastering his affects. His low frustration tolerance became apparent in the *Rosenzweig Picture Frustration Test* (modified by Rauchfleisch, 1979). The

Rorschach Test led to a series of color-determined interpretations that pointed toward preponderantly uncontrolled affectivity. A substantial impairment of the patient's communication ability was also noticed with this test method. Shock phenomena pointed to conflicts in his male identity and in his relationship with women.

This man was in no way ready to recognize an object as such. His intimate friend was his partner and fellow human being only as long as he was willing to fit into the patient's imaginary world. Were his friend to withdraw, he would be killed. It is further obvious that the patient, if he were removed from this fusion with his friend for external reasons, would feel so insecure with women that he (who had already helped to kill one woman) could still not accept their reality and would kill or beat the next one he were to meet.

Thus, it became clear that this patient's epilepsy did not evoke an organic brain disorder. But he was impaired in his self- and his object representations to such an extent that he was only capable of existing if someone were totally submitted to him. If an object withdrew from him or if he feared or had resentments against someone, for example, women, he was not able to deal with it. His only thought was to extinguish reality, to kill the person who did not submit completely to him or even dared to retreat. In our opinion for the court, we wrote that the danger of recidivism was very large. Nevertheless, he did not yet meet the criteria of Art. 42 of the Swiss Penal Code and was therefore declared not to be an habitual criminal, who would have been sent into permanent custody.

It was thought that the testee should be given a chance to undergo a process of maturation and thus gain control over his deep emotions and impulses. We added that Art. 100 of the Swiss Penal Code could be applied, which concerns young adults (from the 18 to 25 years of age), in which case he would be sent to a work detention institute on the premise that this step would prevent further crimes and offences against the law. We recommended that he be treated simultaneously by psychotherapy. Nevertheless, the prognosis had to be considered as very serious.

This example shows that this young man almost exclusively enters into contact with individuals of his own sex, his relationship with them working solely on the basis of fusion. If his "partner" does not correspond to his fantasy, he is not or no longer tolerated as a separate object.

Winnicott (1971) showed how a toddler enters into object relations, primarily in order to destroy the object and to incorporate it into his or her own world, and only upon realizing that it is indestructible is the child capable of a more mature relationship with other human beings, at that time the mother. If a young man like the one we have met felt rejected by the mother from the beginning, he never would have had the chance to develop the intimate relationship that might have enabled him to integrate her into his fantasy. And he was never allowed to experience the warm maternal affection and stimulation that would have given him a healthy self-esteem. He was therefore always aiming for a total fusion with an object, to make up for this early object relationship, as mentioned by Winnicott (1971), and to obtain more self-confidence. By not being able to make up for what he had missed in early childhood, he remained fixated on his unconditional wishes for fusion. Then he could become dangerous to people who—because of their own narcissistic disturbances—were willing to approach him.

Deep anxieties and distrust can appear in individuals who, because of their early childhood experience of neglect, expect the total submission of the object to their own fantasy world—be it through external circumstances, be it because of a genetic insensitivity to stimuli in the environment: When objects retreat from them, even paranoid disorders may arise, which can be very dangerous for those who are getting or have gotten close to them.

A worker in a manufacturing plant was sent to the Basel Psychiatric Outpatient Clinic at age 51 for psychiatric evaluation. Apparently free of hereditary mental diseases, he grew up as the second youngest of seven children, with a affectively reserved mother and a working-class father. From the beginning he was known as a rowdy. At age 11, he had an accident during a school break and broke his right arm. The elbow of this arm remained stiff, so that a major part of the arm and the hand had to be amputated vertically. Nevertheless, he strove to be a craftsman but had difficulties finding a job because of his disability, though he was very skillful in using the rest of his arm and hand together with his healthy hand. At 23 he entered the above-mentioned manufacturing plant and was retrained as a punch-card operator; with great enthusiasm he worked in the data-processing department. At age 31, he voiced serious suspicions against his coworkers and superiors, declaring that they had rummaged through his desk drawers, and he accused a coworker of having been rewarded for this: His superior had finally "shown his true self." In addition, his office neighbors, he complained, were always observing him. He then threatened to do harm to himself or to a coworker. The plant doctor's examination ended in the diagnosis: "Personality disorder with extremely paranoid ideas." The patient was transferred to another department. Tensions arose again when the man was 50 years old. When he noticed that his coworkers were being ordered by his superior to bring some note cards downstairs which he had wanted to keep near his desk, he was infuriated. He beat his superior. It came to a disciplinary action. On psychiatric advice, the action was suspended, as there was great danger that this man would be driven even more deeply into his suspicious attitude. During the psychiatric examination, it was noticed that this man had an incredible desire for recognition, a demanding sense of justice and immense fits of rage as soon as his opinion was not recognized as being right. Those responsible were warned about this—and that he should not be employed any longer in the same department of the manufacturing plant. But they ignored this warning, although not only the medical service but also the plant's management were attuned to the man's dangerous tendencies. Nevertheless, he was reinstated in his old job. Shortly thereafter, he shot his senior chief, after again being overcome by the feeling of having been treated unfairly.

In the test-psychological examinations, it was noted that the patient had an intelligence quotient of 120 according to the German version of the *Wechsler Intelligence Test for Adults* (HAWIE). On the *Rosenzweig Picture Frustration Test* (modified version by Rauchfleisch, 1979), he appeared to be extremely intolerant for frustrations, strongly aggressive toward his environment, and not adapted to the respective situation.

To sum up, it became clear that since childhood—during which he was not yet disabled—this man was disturbed in his means of communication and inclined to dominate his environment through aggressive actions. With an ego prone to fragmentation and with a concomitant narcissistic disturbance, he was unable to develop an empathetic understanding for an object and to introject it. He therefore sought to compensate this deficiency with a total expansion of his remaining narcissism onto objects. This narcissistically severely disturbed man had no feelings of sympathy for others. His superego was only rudimentarily developed, or at best only as an archaic sense of order. And whenever this system of order broke down, his furious will to dominate broke out.

This man was living in the border situation of a person who has difficulties relating to objects, and who is not able to internalize an image of others. Such people have an inadequate object representation, but desire all the more to subsume other people into their authority and power. If the other person resists, violence or even murder can result. These individuals do not tolerate others being far away from them; they have to subdue them or get rid of them. The above-mentioned man with his total narcissistic eagerness to dominate did not tolerate any individuality but his own. He was unable to see objects as they really were. In the sense of Winnicott (1971), he was only able to keep up an object relationship as a subjective imagination of the object, but not to carry on an "object utilization"—for which external reality has to be taken into account. This man was dangerous to people who, for internal or external reasons, got close to him. In one instance it came to a fight, in another to the loss of life. The final reach for the pistol and the destruction of a human life proved his mistaking the inner world with the outer world and destroying anyone who offered resistance. The aggression against such an important person in their lives happens because such people reach a border situation (Battegay, 1981) in which they are narcissistically injured and cannot bear it that the other person is definitively different from themselves, as they cannot sufficiently distinguish such others from themselves and therefore feel threatened by them. Aggression results: They want to put the object that was first considered "good" and then became "bad" out of the way.

> The author had to write an opinion for the court about a 37-year-old woman who shot her drug-addicted husband immediately after his discharge from prison. The asthenic, slender woman was a daughter of a craftsman and a quiet, introverted, cool and severe mother, who worked outside the home since her daughter was 8 years old. She grew up without love in a small row-house the fourth of six children. She had to share her room with a cerebrally disabled brother and another sister. When she was unable to cope with caring for her brother, she was punished. In school she had little difficulties. She was sexually ignorant when she had her first period. After completing her schooling, she took up an artistic profession. She experienced sexual intercourse with her boyfriend as painful and did not want to have anything to do with sex in later relationships. At age 19 she met her future husband, who was somewhat younger than she, in a restaurant preponderantly frequented by drug dependents. He was the first man she really loved. At first, she did not feel anything during sexual intercourse, but later she obtained satisfaction from sex. Her parents were against this relationship. This young woman and her boyfriend traveled together throughout many foreign countries, and for the first time she took drugs. Her boyfriend drank excessively and took amphetamines as well as LSD and heroin. Several times he came in conflict with the law. At the age of 21 she gave birth to a daughter. First, the child was given to a foster family, then into a day-care center. Since she and her friend were out of work, they could keep the child at home. Later she worked in a factory and was very appreciated there as a good worker. But more and more she suffered because her boyfriend did not behave as she expected him to. He took great liberties, inviting girlfriends to their

home and inducing her to become a prostitute to finance his drug consumption. He bought a number of weapons and taught her how to shoot. She felt more and more restricted and deeply disappointed. He tormented her—although he himself had girlfriends—with scenes of jealousy because he could not bear her not being totally dependent on him. She too grew more and more suspicious about him, because not only did he not comply with her expectations, he even trampled on them. Actually, both similarly wanted their partner to live according to their own unconscious tendencies. Her friend was once again put in jail because of a drug offence. At that time they got married. She tried to get him out of prison and got involved herself in a criminal affair. Shortly, she had an extramarital relationship in order (as she told it) to motivate her husband to move out. One day she heard that her husband would come home from prison the next day. The whole night long she thought about what to do and came to the conclusion to kill him because he would never let her go. Thus, on the day of his return she shot him several times with his own weapon.

The whole life story of this young woman shows, on the one hand, that as a child she was not able to get her way, yet on the other hand, she never received the warmth, stimulation and the possibilities for cognitive experiences a child absolutely needs to build up a consistent self and object representation. In her weakness and narcissistic need for fusion, she attached herself to a man who himself had a weak ego and was severely disturbed narcissistically, expecting of him a life in total symbiosis. She became his accomplice in his drug consumption and his escape from prison. On the one hand, she felt that in order to live her own life she had to get away from her husband; on the other hand, in her weakness and insufficiency she was unable to do so. Also, she realized that her husband would not let her go. Thus, she did not feel able to live without the total dominating extension of her narcissism to her husband, but also she could not go on living with him: So she got rid of him. Only by "extinguishing" the object did she believe herself capable of reaching the inner freedom she had not had until then. In the border situation she realized that this man, who was unfaithful and disorderly, would never be at her disposal—despite her watchfulness and although (or even because) he wanted her for his own narcissistic reinforcement and to strengthen his own ego. So she destroyed the object, in the unconscious assumption of thus eliminating the object that had resisted her perception of the world.

A 30-year-old woman who had stolen objects in self-service shops for which she had no use whatsoever was sent by the court to the Basel

Psychiatric Outpatient Department. This woman had grown up under unfavorable family conditions. Her parents were divorced when she was 1 year old. Up to her fourth year of life she lived with her maternal grandparents. When her mother got married again in a distant country, she was brought there. Her stepfather always told her that she did not really belong to the family. She developed a terrible hatred of her own father because he did not care for her. She experienced her mother as weak. Toward her half-sister she reacted with jealousy, and she longed for love, warmth, and security, which she could not get, however. Already as a child she started stealing small amounts of money. She bought sweets for other children, to win them over for herself. After finishing school, she took up pickpocketing and thus got into trouble at her apprenticeship job. Thereafter, she attempted suicide for the first time. To get away from home, she married a man she didn't love. Immediately she yearned for a child, in order to find self-fulfillment and to fill up her inner void. Following a stillbirth, she again attempted suicide. The marriage failed. After the divorce, she immediately took up a relationship with another man. When she discovered that he was a pimp, she made yet another suicidal attempt and had to be brought to a psychiatric hospital. Then she met a man from a foreign country and fell in love with him, but soon he left her burdened with debts. She started to commit thefts, the number of which gradually increased, and it came to repeated fraud and document forgery followed by sentencing. Finally, she began a friendship with an academic. She got pregnant by him and gave birth to a child. This relationship was plagued by repeated tensions. She longed for his love, but he did not give her what she expected. He was always asking himself whether he should stay with her or not, as he felt himself robbed of his freedom by her permanent suspicion. One evening he went out with a male friend living in the same house. She heard the neighbor coming home at 2 a.m., but her friend was not yet there. When he arrived home at 4 a.m., she reproached him for coming home so late. He purportedly answered: "This is a man's business." She then got a kitchen knife and suddenly stabbed him several times in the breast. Soon afterwards he died of the injuries caused by these wounds.

Here we are dealing with a woman with a weak ego and weak self-identity as well as weak object representation who had tried all her life—in vain—to get love from the men she had met and desperately clung to. In some way she expected these men to support her weak self and to take over a complementary function. She could not bear their being independent, and it was not by chance that one of them who fled her went abroad. While living together with the academic, the father of her child, she obviously reached a border situation. Once again she tried to support her weak self and, in a narcissistic collusion, to have a man totally at her disposal, but she could not help but see that he wanted to keep at least a part of his freedom for himself. When she, in her excessive distrust, realized the limited possibilities she had of dominating him, he turned from being a "good" to a "bad" object, and she stabbed him.

In people who are extremely disturbed in their self-representation and their object representation, there is the danger that, because of their fragmentation-prone ego and their tendency toward projective identifications, they can become very seriously suspicious of people close to them and finally reach their limit if they cannot achieve the desired total domination over their partner or another important person. These people can become dangerous not only to themselves, but also to their surroundings.

In this context we have to ask ourselves whether the extended suicide of major depressives is not based on similar dynamics. These patients are often narcissistically totally empty; they no longer experience self-esteem, and their ego as well has become weak because it is no longer narcissistically invested. They cling to someone close, try almost to "incorporate" and to take possession of them (cf. the chapter "Hunger in Depressives and Addicts"). In their complete pessimism, they experience not only themselves, but also their partners or even their own children as doomed. They extend the gloomy ruminations of their unconscious to other objects, and if they decide to commit suicide, they take others with them.

> This was the case with a 45-year-old manager in a large company who had been seeing a psychiatrist for more than a year. He complained about lack of energy, contact difficulties and insomnia, though he also reported that he was still quite able to accomplish his usual work. The psychiatrist prescribed clomipramine, 50 mg in the morning and 50 mg at noon, in addition to the already prescribed trimipramine, 50 mg in the evening, and a benzodiazepine derivative to induce sleep. A week after beginning with this therapy, the patient shot himself one early morning, after having first put a bullet through his wife's head. The two teenage daughters were completely shocked. Their father's act was incomprehensible to them. They reported that he had always been a little reserved and hard-hearted. In the days before his death he had become even more withdrawn.

In this man, narcissistic depletion caused by depression did not allow him to see or bear the object nearest to him as something independent of himself, and—through the antidepressants once again in possession of enough energy and/or now being better able to feel his depressive misery—when he decided to kill himself, he was convinced that the life of his wife would be over, too.

Here, we wonder whether people who are able to do such things because of a fragmentation-prone ego, as the first four examples show, were from the beginning insufficiently capable of feeling the love, warmth and stimulation given them in childhood, and were unable to develop a consistent self and adequate object representations—a true image of themselves and others. It is our conclusion that a certain predisposing genetic component plays a role in the development of such borderline personalities, as witnessed by unloving or emotionally cold characters in the preceding generation; but the miserable milieu of their early childhood may have contributed to making them feel insecure, stifling the development of adequate object representation. When a psychiatrist treats such people, he or she should not disregard the dangers connected with these dynamics. One should consider that these individuals, who aspire for total collusion with their partner (Willi, 1975), intend to destroy the object if it does not perform or behave in the manner expected of it.

If such people are treated psychotherapeutically, it should be considered that the technique used should not be primarily a classical psychoanalytic one: On the one hand, these people initially need a psychotherapy replete with encouragement and recognition; on the other hand, their attention has to be drawn early on to their unrealistic tendencies toward fusion and projective identification, and steered toward seeing and testing outside reality through "expressive, psychoanalytically oriented psychotherapy" according to Kernberg and coworkers (1972). The psychotherapy will, however, only be stabilized after the patients have been convinced—during months or even years of at least one weekly session—of the indestructible therapeutic presence, of the object constancy in the outer world. Therapists, however, should not overestimate their possibilities: If danger emanates from the patient to close others, even with today's more open view of psychiatry, hospitalization to overcome the crisis situation will become inevitable.

As the last example shows, with depressives it is not easy to foresee who will and who will not undergo such a total fusion with an object. Yet in such patients one must be alert to the existence of such a fusion problem, and if it does exist to be ready to work it through psychotherapeutically—in addition to prescribing psychotropic drugs. Hospitalization of such patients at the right time during crisis situations may prevent a fatal development. As in the example described, such tendencies in depressive individuals toward total fantasized fusion often proceed secretly. In such cases, the environment is completely surprised and shocked by the event.

As to their legal responsibility for the criminal acts they committed, with the first four individuals one has to consider that, being of at least average intelligence, they were certainly capable of recognizing the wrongness of their act. But because of their total demand for fusion, they were only partially capable of acting according to this knowledge. In such individuals legal responsibility is thus usually judged as being reduced to a moderate or great extent. Since an individual of average intelligence should be aware of his or her own fusion tendencies and subsequent object dependence from previous life experiences—though not always the unconscious reasons behind them—we cannot consider such persons as completely unresponsible. The prognosis of these people is usually unfavorable, because in the future one can hardly expect a reduction in their fusion demands—unless they receive long-lasting psychotherapy in the described sense in prison. These people usually do not want to be sent to a psychiatric hospital or put in a custodial institution. They generally prefer, if anything at all, to be sent to a normal prison. It is often very striking how little remorse they have over their act. Their superego seems to be immature, capable of assuming little responsibility, or archaically cruel, as Rauchfleisch (1981) has described it for dissocials. It is not experienced as something that regulates, but as something that forbids—something identifying itself more with the surroundings than with themselves. Their only way out then seems to be to cover it up impulsively or to corrupt it.

❖The Hunger of the Diabetic Patient

There are many different forms of diabetes mellitus, whereby genetic, immunological, alimentary, hormonal, and other biochemical factors play varying roles in triggering it. One also speaks of insulin-dependent and insulin-independent diabetes. However, diabetes mellitus may be generated, especially when a high-grade insulin deficiency is present (type I diabetes), the metabolism resembling that of hunger. Diabetics who worry, consciously or unconsciously, about nourishment and have the concomitant fears feel deeply that, despite their greedy efforts to supply the body with food, they are not getting enough. Without therapeutic intervention—without the introduction of homologous insulin—the disturbed sugar metabolism causes especially the carbohydrates not to be metabolized at all or inappropriately. This biochemical situation essentially corresponds to that of hunger.

With respect to the psychoanalytic aspect of diabetes mellitus, Binswanger and Herrmann (1979) mention the hypothesis of "chronic hunger situation." Hinkle et al. (1951, 1952), Bleuler (1954), Alexander (1950) and others remark that some people unconsciously put eating on the same level as love. As the proverb says: "The way to a man's heart is through his stomach." Emotional burdens of various kinds are consciously experienced as love deprivation or as impending love deprivation, and often one has the feeling of having missed some (emotional) "nourishment." The organism may then react as if suffering from hunger. Hinkle and Wolf (1949) hypothesized that diabetics react under emotional strain with ketosis, i.e., with a metabolic reaction specific to the hunger state. Bleuler (1954) speaks of the fact that diabetic metabolism should be understood as hunger metabolism raised to the pathological. Bleuler notes that one can crave not only food, but also appreciation, love, power, etc. Hunger in the one direction could partially be compensated by the stilling of hunger in another realm: An individual who is satiated after a meal would also have the feeling—for the time being—of having satisfied the hunger for success or revenge. A hunger for love or for recognition that is unsatisfied could vicariously be satisfied through excessive eating. Bleuler states, as he admits, somewhat overdrawn: "Could the change of metabolism in hunger states, as is the case in diabetes, be triggered by a figurative hunger, a hunger for love, for being cared for, etc.?" Hinkle and Wolf (1949) hypothesized that diabetes mellitus often results following stress caused by the loss of a person or another object. But this theory does not clarify *why* one individual gets diabetes after stress, whereas another gets a different disease or remains healthy. Groen (1973) assumes that diabetics have often suffered the loss of an important person or of love before the outbreak of their illness. Wilkinson (1981), however, is skeptical about all these statements concerning the psychosomatic origin of diabetes mellitus. He tries to prove that such hypotheses are based on an insufficient or on a biased interpretation of case histories. In this respect we should also recall the work of Dunbar et al. (1936), who described a person predisposed to diabetes mellitus as being weak, irritable, emotionally labile, hypochondriac, often changing his/her behavior, and as someone who is either excessively dependent on other people or who is instead inclined to explosive rebellion. In the author's opinion, these characteristics may perhaps give certain hints for describing the premorbid personality of diabetics, but they cannot be considered as specific traits. Wilkinson emphasizes that in this and similar publications it cannot be judged whether these characteristics actually originated *before* the appearance of diabetes or showed up only *after* the outbreak of the disease. This author correctly states that the emotional trauma caused by the diagnosis of diabetes, especially of the insulin-dependent kind, is indeed usually stronger than that triggered by other chronic diseases. Diabetics, who have to inject themselves with insulin, are—albeit to differing extents— consciously or unconsciously beset with fears, especially in the beginning, even if they have received qualified instructions.

One should also recall that the diabetic has to follow a diet that can actually *stimulate* desires and hunger feelings, even when one fully acknowledges the reason for such measures. "Forbidden fruits," as everyone knows, taste especially good.

A 60-year-old physician who came to the author for psychotherapy, and who did not eat large amounts of food, reported that diabetes mellitus had been diagnosed during his last examination by an internist. He always had liked to eat noodles and other dishes containing flour and other carbohydrates. But now, although he knew that he had to decrease the amounts of such food in his diet, he felt a tremendous demand for these very dishes. He felt "forced" to prepare himself such a meal or have it prepared for him. He did not like these dishes just because they were forbidden, since he had already liked them before; but his awareness that he was no longer able to assimilate the carbohydrates correctly was almost a physical sensation for him, and maybe because of that was he so desirous of those kinds of food and in this respect insatiable, although he otherwise had neither a particular nor a huge appetite. In his behavior lies a certain obstinate resistance against the diet his disease had forced upon him.

There are, however, also diabetics with an acquired aversion to sweets. It is not clear whether this is the direct consequence of the hunger disease or of the severe diet instructions, which represent a sort of object deprivation. To follow a diet means accepting a loss, though it is not clear whether this results directly from noncompliance with the diet and thus the loss of food and of pleasurable feelings connected with its intake. At least until the mourning process is over, the object loss leads to a hunger for taking possession of objects. Gfeller and Assal (1979) spoke of depressive states as reactions occurring after the people concerned have been confronted both with the diagnosis of diabetes mellitus and the necessary mourning process over the loss of health and the impossibility of eating as much as one might like. In this sense diabetics are unsatiated—they are always confronted with foodstuffs they have to renounce. Yet hunger and the degree of satiety are not psychological phenomena completely separated from the somatic substratum; rather, they are the subjective expression of the state of the hypothalamic centers that determine the need for food intake and the experience of satiety. In the chapter on obesity, I pointed out the meaning of the ventromedial hypothalamus as the center of satiety and the ventrolateral hypothalamus as the center of food intake. Cerebral transmitters act as regulators. It is supposed that the sugar metabolism has a direct biochemical effect on these centers.

The author recalls a woman of 65 years, who had lost her mother early in life and therefore grew up with her stepmother. She was educated by her father and her grandparents extremely conscientiously, but did not receive the necessary emotional warmth and love. She always tried to compensate this lack by overeating. When the Germans marched into her native country, she fled with her only child. She experienced a true odyssey until she found a new home in the United States. Later this woman came to Switzerland, since she had found a job here. After the death of her husband, she became very depressive. Also, she developed a serious case of diabetes mellitus. In psychoanalytically oriented therapy, she showed an extremely strong tendency toward self-humiliation. She had insufficient self-assurance and an archaic superego that tortured her. Not seldom the impression arose that, on the one hand, she wanted to punish herself for her feelings of guilt and show her husband how much she felt his loss; but on the other hand, she took offence at his "leaving." The patient reported an extreme "hunger" for emotional care, for statements of love by other persons, which she partly satisfied by excessive food intake. The diabetes, which began after the death of her husband, obviously shows that this attempt at compensating failed.

The more she felt sick (doubtlessly also because of her diabetes), the more she longed for care. She always said she did not feel well alone at home, she felt apathetic, uninterested in life, but she did not want to die; she wondered whether she should begin a university education. On her own she recognized that through this desire for knowledge she was trying to fill up an inner emptiness, that "narcissistic hole" (Ammon, 1974). In such states eating attacks occurred that led to a decompensation of the diabetes, and because of the newly acquired insufficient utilization of carbohydrates eventually to a hunger state. The eating attacks may also point to an autodestructive tendency in the patient which expressed itself in her depression. A vicious circle (deficient self—excessive eating—alimentary diabetes—hunger state of the organism—depression [deficient self]) arose. In her case, it was clear that the blood sugar tests were better when she herself felt better, e.g., when she was together with people who liked, respected and cared for her.

This woman's diabetes, which occurred only after the death of her husband, represents the physical testimony of a hunger for love and attention that remained unsatisfied after the death of her partner. Yet we cannot clearly state that this woman suffered from diabetes mellitus only as a result of the loss of her husband, and that no other hunger disease could have followed: Obviously, the corresponding genetic predisposition must have existed.

Psychological connections between diabetes and hunger cannot be proved. We only have hints that diabetics have excessive tendencies toward (oral) incorporation and narcissistically taking possession of objects, and that these tendencies often become apparent in people who have experienced a loss and who suffer from a more or less distinct hunger for love and care. Luban-Plozza and Pöldinger (1971) even speak of a complete identification of eating with love in diabetics, which would explain their constant hunger.

Nowadays, it cannot be clearly determined whether these theories are correct, especially when one considers that juvenile type I diabetics generally do not correspond to this—hungry—incorporation type and usually do not consume too much food. One also has to consider that autoimmune processes lead to a destruction of the insulin-producing cells in the pancreas and thereby block the utilization of carbohydrates. These are conditions that actually correspond to a hunger in the organism, though generally without causing the feeling of hunger. For this the catabolic metabolism might be responsible that originates in the catabolism of fats instead of carbohydrates. According to Alexander (1950), however, these incorporation impulses manifest themselves in many different ways. Thus, a tendency to refuse food can be followed by increased food desire. This desire can express itself in an insatiable urge for food, in the wish to be constantly nourished and in never-ending demands for fulfillment in interpersonal relationships. These incorporation impulses also reveal themselves, as Alexander sees it, in excessive mother identification with, in consequence, impaired psychosexual development. Although this interpretation seems to be very hypothetical, Alexander and his Chicago group have apparently also observed diabetics who have a low food intake, who even reject dishes, and who thus apparently do not feel extreme hunger and appetite. As mentioned, this behavior can also be interpreted as a consequence of diet instructions, which may cause a hunger patient problems because of the associated object deprivation or object loss. It is, however, known that type II diabetes gets better when the available food is made scarce or when hunger reigns objectively, for example, in war times. Here, one has to consider that these diabetics show a decrease in weight, which means the remaining insulin reserves are once again sufficient: Their metabolism improves. Also, in such times the fate of diabetics is no longer a special one with respect to hunger, so that they then feel relieved.

A sign of the possible significance of a disturbance of the endorphine system or of the endogenous opiates, at least in a subgroup of insulin-independent diabetics, may be found in the fact that after a combined intake of chlorpropamide (oral antidiabetic drug) and alcohol, encephaline (belonging to the endorphine system) shows a significantly higher concentration in the blood of diabetics than in that of healthy people who take the same combination (Medbak et al., 1981).

Since a hunger disease is more or less clearly linked with diabetes mellitus (despite treatment it persists at least latently), the patient cannot simply be put on a diet without further explanation. The people concerned need detailed information on the biochemical and psychological backgrounds as well as the effects of diabetes, and information in line with their emotional needs. Especially group sessions have proved to be effective with diabetics (Gfeller & Assal, 1981; Haenel & Berger, 1984) in which, on the one hand, the patients obtain both facts and guidance, and on the other hand have the chance to discuss their problems related to diabetes, especially the diet, with a doctor, a nurse, a diet consultant and copatients. Close interdisciplinary cooperation and communication between the doctor, the other staff members and the patients is necessary, since only in this way can a therapy be realized that views human beings as psychosomatic entities living in a social system. De Poret and coworkers (1984) from the Hôpital Bichat in Paris have likewise put together therapeutic diabetics groups and worked through their conscious or unconscious problems. Above all, these authors were concerned with achieving an educational effect—a learning process directed at attaining an emotional acceptance of diabetes as well as the necessary treatment and subsequent diet. In the group, it is further possible to give diabetics, who often feel disadvantaged by their disease and are thus unconsciously unsatiated in their oral and narcissistic "hunger," the necessary affective attention to "feed" their selves (again) with more (emotional) human warmth and affirmation. In the group, diabetics too can include each other in their selves, so that, as stated elsewhere (Battegay, 1977), each participant forms a "narcissistic group-self," a "we feeling," and an identification with the others on this basis. In group work these patients have the opportunity to support each other and to help each other to work through their narcissistic-oral deficiencies.

❖Gastrointestinal Disturbances as the Expression of a Hunger Disease

As early as 1950, Alexander noted that emotional factors are very important in the etiology of gastrointestinal disturbances. In babies one can see that the absence of oral satisfaction* and thus hunger lead to feelings of displeasure and to crying. Through their sounds children unconsciously try to motivate the mother or another important person to feed them. Children who are not satisfied will remain hungry. Whether or not a child is breast-fed by the mother seems not to be as important for the act of nourishment as the warmth offered the child at the mother's breast. The actual food can easily be substituted by artificial products—the contact of the child's mouth with the mother's nipple and skin cannot: An infant who has to be fed artificially because the mother lacks milk can still be pressed to the mother's breast in the same way and be hugged. Not the physical food is crucial, but the warmth and stimulation obtained by touching the mother's skin. One should not cause guilt feelings in mothers who are unable to breast-feed their children; rather, one should show them how they can offer the necessary emotional attention by hugging the infant. Certainly in this sense the child needs maternal "nourishment."

Alone the filling of the stomach leads to a feeling of pleasure, and when children do not feel this pleasure they cry in a demanding and increasingly unhappy manner, indicating their desperate need for food. In the long run, even when otherwise optimal care and nourishment are offered, children do not thrive who do not experience sufficient emotional nourishment. Spitz's observations (1965) in an orphanage of 91 babies who were looked after by nurses, each of whom each had to care for more than 10 children, prove how important emotional attention in childhood is. Of the 91 infants observed, 34 (37%) died in the course of 2 years, although they were physically well fed. Humans do not live by bread alone, but even more so by warm love. Without tender loving care human babies cannot develop properly. If one does not

---

*   Grinker (1953) stated that, on the perceptive level, orality also serves to further Gestalt impressions and thus the proper evaluation of external objects as well as inner contentment.

experience such emotional warmth as a child, one will search for emotional "nourishment" throughout one's life. Children who have learned to swallow, as it were, only their own saliva will suffer forever from emotional hunger.

> A woman of 28 years, who grew up together with three brothers and sisters in very educated surroundings in a neighboring country, felt completely neglected in her early childhood, especially by her mother. In those days, it was her experience that her mother's intellectual interests took precedence over her own education. She had to content herself with nannies, who were more or less capable of looking after her, but never gave her enough emotional warmth. Since childhood she sometimes felt pains in the epigastrium (which she considered stomach pains), especially when she was not able to bear emotionally stressful experiences. She was not conscious of her emotional problems and described preponderantly the physical pains. At such times she was unable to experience hunger and did not eat enough. Her hunger for emotional care appeared particularly in her relationship with her husband and children. In her fantasy she more or less completely fused with them. Perhaps this explains why she did not eat—despite her enormous emotional hunger or perhaps because of it. Maybe her "hunger" was satiated by her husband, who took great emotional interest in her feelings, but in the end he was not able to satisfy her needs, and her hunger could be understood as a manifestation of an emotional deprivation.

As mentioned, the patient had little knowledge of her feelings of frustration, which according to Sifneos (1973) is typical for psychosomatically afflicted people. She could not "feel" her emotions and suffered from alexithymia (the inability to "read" feelings). It is probably not by chance that her psychosomatic ailments were linked to the stomach, though other hunger patients may suffer from completely different symptoms linked to other organs. To date, direct correlations between certain psychodynamics and a special organ system have not been determined. Predispositional factors and the value an organ has in a person's and/or a family's value system also play a role, but as Luban-Plozza and Pöldinger (1971) state, it is certain that the human need for security and protection is important in the origin of gastrointestinal disturbances. In this context, the question arises as to what extent even extreme forms of gastrointestinal disturbances, for example, gastrointestinal cancers, originate in the insecurity provoked by a new situation experienced as insolvable. There are many reports from cancer patients indicating that their condition began after a disturbing experience that caused a feeling of existential insecurity and/or a devaluating, narcissistic injury.

As Luban-Plozza and Pöldinger (1971) emphasize, patients who suffer from stomach or duodenal ulcers are usually deficient in working through life events, whereby it is our understanding that both the psychological *and* the physical syndromes are expressions of a hunger disease. In this sense, it is important for the treating physician to recognize the emotional correlations of these diseases.

A 17-year-old adolescent suddenly complained of pains in the middle and left epigastrium, generally arising about 5 hours after meals. The pain occurred more promptly and intensively after alcohol and coffee consumption. He was under the constant care of a gastroenterologist up to and during the treatment at our Psychiatric Outpatient Clinic at the age of 24. A duodenal ulcer had been detected by X-ray when he was 17.

The patient is the son of a foreigner, a very skillful craftsman who, despite his small earnings, had saved a fortune. However, at the time when the patient first felt these pains, his father had already been mentally ill for some 5 years—he had gone through episodes of a bipolar affective psychosis and was very difficult to treat, especially in the manic phase. The patient's mother, 5 years younger than the father, came from the same village as the father and was also a very skilled craftswoman. She added substantially to the family fortune. The patient also has a brother 5 years his younger.

On the one hand, the patient felt himself to be a "child of love"; on the other hand, his parents were very occupied by their professions, which meant that from the age of 2 on he had to stay with another family during the daytime. The woman in the day-care family was also a foreigner, but she had no children. Generally, the patient felt well in these surroundings. But two experiences remained in his memory: Once the woman stayed in bed all morning, after his father had brought him to her. All of a sudden, he urgently needed to go to the potty, but the woman didn't come to put him on it. Finally, he wet the bed. At that time he was already toilet trained. The incident caused a great narcissistic injury. The second event he still sees, he said, vividly before his eyes: The woman laid him on her own bed. He began to move about and jump on the bed, until she pushed him off with a foot. He fell to the ground. He experienced this event as a great injustice, although he had since repeatedly tried to forgive her. From then on he did not feel secure there.

In kindergarten he felt mistreated by a nun: He simply did not want to behave as she had ordered it. At the age of 14 or 15 years he complained that his parents thought only about their work. Between his 16th and 19th year of life he was friends with a woman a year older than himself. But at age 24 he had still not had an intimate relationship with a woman. He noticed that he was always struggling for recognition. Earlier, he had felt injured in many situations, more than others. He had experienced few stimuli and hardly any encouragement through his parents. His father's illness weighed heavily on him. He did not want to have the image of his very capable mother in mind when looking for a woman.

The patient was a law student and stated that his role model for the profession was a lawyer he knew. He said that he took up the study of law not only for objective reasons, but maybe also for materialistic reasons.

During psychotherapy it became apparent that the patient had enormous expectations of his conversational partner. Somehow he—hungrily—expected to get from the other person the self-confidence he himself did not have. He also reported that his brother was very successfully learning to be a craftsman, whereas he was having some difficulties with his studies—he had had to repeat a preliminary examination. During the conversations with the patient, the impression arose that although he received considerable attention, he nevertheless remained "hungry." It also became apparent that he found excuses for all his parents' actions, even for their mistakes. One could see in his eyes that he was emotionally very affected; but it was also obvious that he was able to recognize and to express his feelings only to a very small degree. Sifneos (1973) described this, as mentioned, as the "alexithymia" of psychosomatic patients—their incapacity to "read" and recognize their feelings. This patient obviously fostered enormous expectations of the people he encountered, and yet emotionally he was left almost empty-handed because nobody was able to correspond to them. In this respect, the duodenal ulcer could (also) be seen as one result of his hunger disease.

People who have long-term "hungering" expectations—which always contain tendencies toward incorporation and narcissistic wishes for fusion—hardly ever have the chance to be satisfied or to be satiated. Nevertheless, or perhaps for that very reason, it is understandable that they seem to produce more digestive juices than the average population. Mirsky (1958, 1961/1962) examined 2073 recruits concerning pepsinogen and determined the normal distribution relative to the pepsinogen concentration in blood. He chose a group of 63 hypersecretors from the 300 men (15%) with the highest rates of pepsinogen; the group of hyposecretors consisted of 57 of the 719 men (19%) with the lowest concentration of pepsinogen. Following thorough gastrointestinal X-ray examinations and various psychological tests, the men went to the training camp. All but 13 were examined psychologically and radiologically in a follow-up study between the 8th and the 16th week of their basic training. The first X-ray examination at the beginning of recruit training showed a completely healed duodenal ulcer in 3 and an active ulcer in 1 of the 63 men with gastric hypersecretion. The second X-ray examination in the 8th to the 16th week revealed an active duodenal ulcer in 5 more men who had not show signs of any gastrointestinal disturbance at the beginning of the research project. But all individuals who had a duodenal ulcer or had meanwhile developed one belonged to the 63 men with a high serum pepsinogen rate. All 9 ulcer patients belonged to the group of the 15% with the highest blood pepsinogen concentration; 8 of them represented the highest 5%.

According to this—controversial—study, individuals with a high concentration of pepsinogen in the blood are clearly more ulcer prone than people with less pepsinogen in blood.

Mirsky (1958, 1961/1962) did another, longer term study on 1600 children from the age of a few months up to 16 years, and on 4460 adult men and women from various socioeconomic classes. Of these, the 2% with the highest serum pepsinogen concentration were taken together as a group of hypersecretors and were specially examined. Similarly, the 2% with the lowest rates were selected to be a group of hyposecretors. Although the study was not yet completed, the author reported already that a great number of the previously healthy hypersecretors who were observed over several years developed the symptoms of a duodenal ulcer, which was then proved with X-ray as well. In contrast, none of the individuals in the hyposecretors group developed a duodenal ulcer. Of the 2% of the children with the highest serum pepsinogen concentration, 10% developed a duodenal ulcer at the age of 4-6 and 10-14 years, respectively.

Mirsky's results would confirm the opinion that gastric and duodenal ulcer are due, among other pathogenic factors such as infection, to "hunger" in the designated sense. Whatever emotional care and material "food" they receive, it would not be enough. Ulcer patients remain insatiable apparently because orally they expect more than they get or can experience. Hence, they would correspond to the criteria for individuals who are fixated on the oral level of development.

Gastric and duodenal ulcers are occasionally found in alcohol dependents before their excessive drinking begins, as Labhardt (1964) states. Labhardt points out that the ulcers therefore cannot be considered the *effect* of chronic alcohol intake; rather, gastric and duodenal ulcers and alcohol dependence result, at least partly, from the same basic disease. Both can be said to represent symptoms of the underlying hunger disease.

As Melanie Klein (1935) maintains, such individuals pursue the total object that might completely satisfy them. Since it is impossible to realize this intention, they remain hungry and accordingly have too much pepsinogen. This search for a total object occurs not only because of the desire for (oral) incorporation, but also because of their desire for an object with which a fusion and symbiosis can take place. As the example of the young ulcer patient shows, these people might not only be orally fixated, but also narcisstically impaired in their narcissism, their self— people who try, insatiably and therefore in vain, to strengthen themselves or their selves through a fusion with others. Even in regard to these narcissistic needs they are condemned to remain "hungry," because an enduring fusion with the object is usually not possible.

Mirsky is right in pointing out that, besides the assumed genetic factors (proved by Rotter et al., 1979, through immunological examinations), doubtlessly, among other factors, also typical psychological constellations and social realities contribute to the development of ulcers. Regarding the psychological factors, we have already pointed out the insatiable "hunger" of these people through which they become dependent on their surroundings and then try to compensate for their fusionary dependence tendencies via overactivity. Alexander (1950) considered the denial of the person's desires for support, help and love as the main factor in the pathogenesis of gastric and duodenal ulcers.

The social factors involved are always such that these individuals, who are constantly on the outlook for security, become very tense when something is expected of them by the outside world. Especially in situations in which their talents as leaders are required do their desires to be cared for emerge. Such people, who more than others long for safety and attention, seem to want to escape these tendencies, though it is impossible to neglect such wishes of being cared for without due "punishment." They result from earlier experiences of neglect, through which the people concerned insatiably demand constant new compensations through attestations of love and exhibition of warm feelings. Although or perhaps because these people are unaware of their infantile wishes for security, they unconsciously defend themselves against them by an especially strong attitude of self-confidence. Perhaps one could generally say that people who work untiringly in their social functions are in effect constantly fleeing their profound and deep wishes for loving care as well as the depressive feelings resulting from the frustration of these tendencies. They desire—no doubt insatiably—to "get" this needed recognition and emotional "food" that will ultimately make them able to forget their narcissistic deficiencies. Besides the fact that such a compensation of narcissistic deficiencies is impossible regardless of the amount of approval and appreciation granted, the true fulfillment of such narcissistic needs would rob these people of the motives for their constant activities.

❖Cardiovascular Disorders and Inhibited Hunger for Action

As Alexander (1950) emphasized, today there can be no doubt that emotional factors play an important role in the development and maintenance of essential hypertension and coronary diseases. Friedman and Rosenman's inquiries (1974) into the causes of coronary diseases and myocardial infarction, in which type-A (higher risk) and type-B (lower risk) personalities were defined, have gained worldwide recognition. The authors found that some people fight an excessive and relatively chronic battle to reach an unlimited number of goals or objects in their surroundings within the shortest time—even against all obstacles or extensive efforts by other people. These people, labeled type-A personalities, live in a constant vicious circle of emotion and action. They are always busy and try to do continually ever more in an ever shorter time. The type-A individual thereby tries to overcome and dodge these burdens constantly. Such people, who are trying to take possession of and to incorporate ever more objects and/or to find repeated recognition by others, could be seen as people who are constantly "hungry." Friedman and Rosenman (1974) see the type-A behavior pattern as typical for modern society: Our society gratifies those who think more, achieve more and enter into more active and more aggressive contact with other people. This fact stimulates type-A individuals even more to their kind of behavior. As they note, the type-A personality is strong, vivid, courageous, with forceful body movements, someone who clenches the fists during an ordinary conversation. The fast, explosive manner of speaking on one hand and the impatience on the other hand cause them to adopt the irritating habit of continuing sentences for others or condensing their own sentences. According to these authors, approximately 10% of the urban population show extreme type-A behavior. These people have an above-average concentration of cholesterol, triglycerides and serum B lipoproteins in the blood. If they receive adrenocorticotropic hormone (ACTH), they have a lower 17-hydroxycorticosteroid concentration in their urine than type-B individuals—apparently because ACTH release is permanently increased through their overactivity and their constant overworking of their adrenocortical system, which leads to a reduced availability of 17-hydroxycorticosteroids and therefore to a lower urine concentration of these metabolites. If type-A personalities feel challenged, their norepinephrine secretion is increased, whereas type-B individuals do not show such reactions.

Rosenman et al. (1975/1976) reported a follow-up study comprising 8 1/2 years which included 3500 men between the age of 39 and 59 who were occupied in 10 California firms. In 257 of these employees, clinically diagnosed coronary disease emerged during this prospective study. Type-A behavior was highly significantly correlated with coronary disease ($p<0.0001$ – $p<0.003$). Type-A behavior was not correlated with age, height, body weight, heredity, the cigarette smoking, blood pressure or serum cholesterol and triglyceride concentration.

Friedman and Rosenman (1974) also observed that the type-A personality represents a special risk factor greater than all others or at least equal to the other factors under discussion. It even became clear that type-A personalities show a frequency of myocardial infarction and angina pectoris which is approximately double that of others. Friedman and Rosenman (1974) state that type-A individuals always try to meet the challenges. Yet these people suffer from a deep feeling of insecurity, which causes them to undertake unrealistic attempts at dominating all situations. The described "hunger" (or in English the "thirst") for action would therefore arise out of self-insecurity, i.e., a narcissistic deficiency. Inevitably, they demand too much of their body, since they can succeed only temporarily tranquilizing their inner insecurity, despite the fact that they do chalk up an increasing number of external successes.

Ursula Engelhardt (1979) examined 52 children from 7 to 15 years (24 boys and 28 girls) with orthostatic disturbances of circulation and 51 children of a control group via clinical psychiatric and test-psychological means. She observed that the children with orthostatic disturbances of circulation have a high overall performance-oriented motivation. Their desire for success is not less pronounced, but their fear of misfortune is much higher than in the control group.

Henry and Stephens (1977) state that the type-A personalities correspond to a high degree to the dominant animals in mammalian societies which are constantly challenged to defend their positions in front of rivals. One might say that they are people—or in the realm of mammalian societies, animals—who through their hunger for power fight their fear of falling into an unfavorable position. Henry (1976) had the impression that the behavior of formerly isolated animals in a social system runs parallel to the behavior of type-A individuals in human society: These animals are extremely active, hostile and agitated. Although their plasma corticosterol shows normal values in their young years, when they grow older they have higher than average blood pressure and catecholamine values. A dominant monkey or a dominant mouse shows a lower reaction of the adrenocorticotropic hormone than a subordinate animal. This situation would be similar to that of type-A individual. The type-B personality is said to have no sense of hurry, to be always patient and not to always feel forced to achieve.

If we consider what we have just said about the type-A personality, we can note that there seems to be a more or less pronounced narcissistic deficiency at the basis of this restless activity and the insatiable hunger for action. In our society especially those people are motivated to achieve who thus tend to compensate for their deficient self and their insufficient self-security. Many prominent business managers, university professors, high ranking military officers, and last but not least politicians are type-A personalities, and they try to compensate their narcissistic deficiency through constant activity. Perhaps this is also the reason why such personalities generally have the impression of not receiving enough recognition and not reaching a high enough position of power. In this respect they remain more or less unsatiated and always desire more—until they reach the limits of their capabilities to perform, or until they suffer from a coronary disease—or in politics until they become unbearable for their people.

A business man who had had a myocardial infarction at age 40 and had now, at age 48, been depressive for 2 months consulted the author. His father and his brother had been deported by the Nazis, and his mother had died young, most probably from grief. Up to the age of 19, he had lived together with his family and was then separated from them, which saved him from deportation to a concentration camp. Since childhood he has been very ambitious and had already finished his law studies with honors at the age of 23. First, he worked in his native country as a civil servant, and afterwards he led the large retail business his father had originally founded. At the age of 28 he married a woman 6 years his senior. The marriage remained childless. The patient enlarged his business constantly to become the most important one in the city in which he lived. When he consulted the author, a new building that was to double his business capacity was about to be completed. The patient suffered repeatedly from coronary disturbances and visited the author at irregular intervals for psychotherapy. The depression could be elucidated by an—analytically oriented—psychotherapy in combination with antidepressants. In the fourth year of his psychotherapy, a coronarography revealed a generalized coronary sclerosis. The patient had to undergo bypass surgery, and as he told me on the telephone some months later, he felt better afterwards and suffered remarkably less coronary symptoms. Depressions had no longer occurred.

As is typical for type-A behavior, this man, perhaps as a result of the deportation of his father and brother, was quite insecure and tried to expand his business activities more and more to prove his efficiency both to himself and to others. He could never do enough work, he constantly had to expand his radius of activity in order to stand his ground in his own eyes— and to receive the attention of his (motherly) wife and the rest of his environment. In his own opinion he never did enough. He was always trying to prove his own self-value by ever more successes. That he was putting more than enough strain on himself was visible not only in his coronary sclerosis, but also in his depression, which also reveals his overdemanding attitude toward himself. The depression showed that he experienced his enormous expectations toward himself and toward his environment as unsatisfactory, yet at the same time they led to his receiving the desired attention—at least in the scope of his illness.

People who suffer from hypertension carry within themselves, as Alexander (1950) says, a chronic inhibited aggressivity, always connected with anxiety, which leads to high blood pressure through overactivity of the sympathetic nervous system with an increased heart-minute volume, vasoconstriction as well as release of renin. Renin itself results in the transformation of angiotensinogen into the blood-pressure-increasing substance angiotensin. Although among high blood pressure patients there are also those with a low renin concentration, especially in the elderly (Bühler et al., 1975), the fact remains that in patients with hypertension, although consisting of various personality types (Perini et al., 1982), a common characteristic can be observed: their incapacity to freely express their aggressive impulses. They are usually very controlled and only rarely dare to contradict their conversation partner. Mostly they are very ambitious, but their compliant attitude often causes them to retreat, which makes them angry and hurts their self-respect—which was already deficient—even more. Such people suffering from hypertension do not correspond exactly to type-A personalities with their overactivity and aggressivity, which they transform into actions and external success. They meet rather the criteria of a type-B personality drawn by Friedman and Rosenman (1974). Exceptionally, we find, however, among people with hypertension type-A individuals as well who seem to be successful and expand their field of activity more and more. Apparently, the inhibition of aggressivity in these people does not encompass all parts of their experiences and behavior.

A physician of 55 years consulted the author. It was striking how difficult he found it to describe why he had really come. He only said that his psychological problems were enormous. Two years ago his wife had run off with another man. Thereafter, he (together with his wife) went for a short time for psychological testing, but she was still living together with the other man in a neighboring village. He had to bring up the three children of 12, 16 and 18 years by himself and do his work as well. For a year he had a friendship with a woman 20 years his junior who was divorced from her first husband and had two children. They discussed her and her two children (of 12 and 14 years) moving in with him. To date, though, they had not realized this because his wife repeatedly came into the house. His father was 84 years old, a retired civil servant. The mother had died a year ago. Up to the age of 24 the patient had been a prisoner of war. He had to repeat the examination for matriculation, and he then completed his studies in the shortest possible time. After 2 years as an assistant in a hospital, he opened his own practice. More and more patients came to him, and he furnished several rooms in his practice in order to examine and treat his patients. He walked from room to room to look after his patients almost all day long, and he made house visits as well. Furthermore, he had to look after his children.
I had the impression that, following the separation from his wife, the patient was in a constant struggle to master—alone and without rebellion—the new tasks and increased demands made on him, for example, the impending divorce process. He had not even tried to take a lawyer for himself, intending to quietly master this task, too. The patient suffered from a hypertension of 220/110 mmHg, apparently already for several months. He not only made the impression of being very tense, rigid, full of inhibited aggressions, and taciturn, but also hungry for recognition, benevolence, encouragement, and acknowledgement. About his childhood he said that his mother had been overprotecting: "I was everything for my mother." But now, he said, he was emotionally very locked up and had not been able to give his wife much attention. He went on: "She then took on friends. She was in search of more love." The patient, suffering not only from hypertension, but also from bronchial asthma at least for 2 years, proved to be severely disturbed

narcissistically. He apparently was constantly searching for the acknowledgement he had received abundantly in his early life, but was unable to express his need verbally. Primarily, he was spoiled and overadaptive, and secondarily he was frustrated and inhibited concerning his aggressions. He was unable to give his wife loving care and attention mainly because he was looking only for a narcissistic fusion with her, yet he hardly ever showed her his feelings for her.

It was not by chance that this man suffered from essential hypertension. After his wife had moved out, he lived alone with his children, yet he was unable to describe them adequately. The only person he could really describe colorfully was his 84-year-old father, a retired civil servant whom the patient regularly visited. His father had been very strict with him after his return from the war and made him take up the studies he had started before the war. Almost incidentally, the patient told about his occasional asthma attacks, especially when he felt under stress and unable to resist pressures put on him. Under medical treatment his hypertension improved to 150/100 mmHg. But the patient remained tense, always trying to "mend the holes" that opened up in his existence and to master unforeseen situations without bemoaning his fate.

This patient tried to be master of all vicissitudes—and to accomplish his professional work without interruption. He always adapted himself to the given situation, was constantly looking for acknowledgement, but never seemed to receive any. In his "hunger" for attention and emotional nourishment as well as for narcissistic fusion, he gave the impression of being unsatiated. (He is also obese.) During psychotherapy, he constantly waited to get something from the therapist. Because he apparently did not receive enough attention for himself, he stopped coming after three consultations, owing the author his fee for a very long time.

This patient corresponded to the inhibited aggression of the individuals with hypertension described by Alexander (1950). In his professional life he was ambitious, but he was able neither to show nor to express his wishes and feelings for his wife. Also, he adapted himself constantly to his personal circumstances, which were getting more and more difficult. Thus, he was still so tolerant toward his wife (who after all had left him) that she could come into the house whenever she wanted, and he felt obliged not to take his woman friend into the house. This constant adaptation to the demands of his environment led not only to externally visible muscular tension, but also to the constant mobilization of his inner defensive powers—and certainly in the consequence to his hypertension. It was characteristic of him that he could hardly accept this inner struggle, not experiencing his life at all very consciously, so that he also felt only few aggressions toward the outer world.

People suffering from hypertension are often individuals who are actually quite ambitious, but who always put aside their ambitions when they have to act aggressively to get ahead. They try to, or feel obliged to, adapt if at all possible to the demands of people they are in contact with. They are individuals who in their early childhood experienced either not enough love or rather overprotection, or they always had to correspond to parents' expectations. Especially the latter, who always had to behave ideally, developed an ideal self, but failed to obtain a real or true self, and thus remain unable to take an aggressive stance. They are inhibited to such an extent that they are unable to even realize their desires, and for this reason alone they develop an inner tension and, through the above-mentioned biochemical mechanisms, hypertension.

❖Emotional Hunger in Life-Threatening Situations by Serious Illness

In everyday life we develop defenses against the fact that we can get ill and die. One lives as if able to act and function for eternity. The illusion of being able to partake eternally of earthly life gives us the motivation for ambitious efforts and deeds. But if a serious, dangerous, or even life-threatening ailment comes upon us, then anxieties occur. We are—often unexpectedly—confronted with the fact that many possibilities have not yet been realized.

Like most human beings, such individuals have, up to that time, not developed certain fundamentally relevant realms of their personality. In recognizing a serious physical danger, they realize that their neglect may be final. As Elisabeth Kübler-Ross (1973), Herzig (1978) and other authors have stated, people who have just learned about their serious illness tend to deny the true physical jeopardy. They first do not believe that their cancer or some other serious disease is true, and they shut out the course of disease from their experience, even when they have been instructed about the nature of the ailment. Somewhere in their mind, however, they know that it is a serious matter, but they largely put their being sick out of their thoughts. Nevertheless, or even for this reason, these individuals need contact with a physician. Indeed, they are often even "hungry" for an exchange of thoughts with a doctor, not the least because they have no one else to talk with about their problems. This "hunger" to speak with a physician should not be ignored by the doctor, as these people would otherwise suffer greatly from their emotional isolation and need, despite the fact that they more or less consciously or unconsciously try to fight it. The physician should be available to these patients for talks since they usually do not persist in their tendency toward denial and soon want to talk more realistically about their illness and the prognosis thereof. In the first phase, which Elisabeth Kübler-Ross (1973) called the "denial stage," they deny the truth and make plans for the future they would not make if they were fully conscious of their serious illness. Listening to such patients in such moments one would not think they were indeed seriously ill: Once again their hunger for life is stirring enormously. One often gains the impression that they want to convince the physician (and nature) to keep the illness at bay. In these moments, it becomes obvious that Freud's (1920) notion of a death instinct in humans does not correspond to reality. Especially such people, who are closer to death and have to face it more directly than others, often do not want anything more ardently than to be allowed to continue living. If people who learn about their serious physical condition commit suicide, this is not proof that their acts in fact support the hypothesis of a death instinct. Rather, they simply cannot imagine living a disabled, painful or continually endangered life: They do not want or are not able to face this menace and thus commit suicide. It is therefore not the death instinct that leads them to commit suicide, but the fact that they are not able to live out their *life instinct*. Indeed, they still experience a hunger for life, but they consider the chance of further satisfying it as low or not given.

When talking to patients who are in this denial phase, the physician recognizes that when they change the subject, they are wanting to devote themselves to more pleasant thoughts. Hope and a hunger for life are stirring within the patient. Not rarely do we hear that such an individual has had a recent dream of healthy life, and we should recall that there have been patients whose future imaginations of this kind have—against all prognosis—actually become true. The negation of reality is usually only a passing phase, but it shows that these individuals are still entirely fixated on life and have a hunger for more experiences. Patients who deny their ailment right up to their death are, of course, known to every physician, but they are the exception: They are people who could never endure reality because they did not have the necessary ego strength and self-consistency, and probably because of their unfulfilled hunger for life as well, since in their ego weakness and self-deficiency they did not get enough out of life. It would be wrong to force the truth upon them, since they might break under it. But again, these patients are not as common as often thought.

Most patients do not deny their illness for very long. They occasionally feel the need for a real human contact with a doctor and to talk about their ailment openly. They are hungry for this form of human participation which they are not able to receive from anyone else. It is therefore necessary for the physician to confront these people and to inform them accordingly. An example of a patient the author has written about elsewhere (Battegay, 1979) is quoted here:

106

A woman of 42 years came to see the author after having been depressive for years and not being able to emotionally work through her illness, a lymphogranulomatosis. She was 20 years old when she learned about it. At that time she had been married for one year, and shortly before had given birth to a daughter. The patient, who in her early childhood had to flee her home country together with her parents and come to Switzerland at the age of 11, was never able to experience the love and care she needed, neither during the flight nor later in a foster family nor with her parents. The mother behaved tyrannically and showed little love, the father cared more about his business than about his family. This woman's husband was 14 years her senior and did not show much understanding for her. As a young mother she started to sense a lymph gland on the neck, and a physician eventually diagnosed lymphogranulomatosis. The patient, however, was not informed. But during an X-ray examination, she accidentally saw the diagnosis of "Morbus Hodgkin." She looked up this disease in an encyclopedia and discovered, at that time 20 years old, that this illness had an unfavorable prognosis. She then went home and wanted to discuss her problem with her husband. He was unapproachable and wanted to turn her over to her parents. But she did not allow this and from then on lived separated from him, together with her little daughter. The patient had extreme sleep troubles, did not keep up human contacts, and waited to die. But radiotherapy had a positive therapeutic result: Recidivisms could be treated, and eventually she no longer had any relapses. At the age of 42, she could not bear it any longer alone at home. Her daughter was then 19 years old, and the two of them could not stand each other. The daughter experienced her mother as being a tyrant and suffered herself from various anxieties. The patient, although working half-days as a medical assistant, was so disturbed in her ability to make contact with others that in her free time she listened to the sounds of the neighbors in order to satisfy her hunger for life and to keep up a certain contact with life around her. Her physician, who had treated her for years, was interested in her situation, but was not able to get her away from centering solely on herself. The insufficient orientation at the beginning of the disease led to the patient's withdrawal from all communicative situations, and only when she could no longer stand it did she come for psychotherapeutic help. The psychotherapy, which took place individually and in groups, lasted for several years. Only slowly did she succeed in emerging from her total concentration on her disease. Her hunger for life dawned again, and step by step she started entering into human relationships again.

This example shows the importance of an appropriate orientation of a patient. This patient did not deny her disease, as is so often the case; but she classified the—accidentally discovered—diagnosis as a mark of death and withdrew more or less completely from reality. Her hunger for life made itself known only in her taking notice of sounds in her neighborhood. Through psychotherapy she succeeded in directing her hunger for life toward other human beings.

Even when patients at first do not accept their disease, they are eventually confronted with it through its progression. Then the situation occurs in which the patients are consumed by anger. In his book *Mars*, Fritz Zorn (1977) (this pseudonym means in German "anger") showed very eloquently how great his resentment was toward his disease and toward his parents after he had learned about his serious condition—and after he had profoundly experienced how "unlived" his life still was and how strong his hunger for life was.

Patients fight the fatality of their destiny and may ask why they have been stricken by this fate. In this phase, it is difficult for the families, the physicians, and the nurses to enter into contact with the patients. Patients will say that their physicians are not worth much and have actually endangered them through false diagnosis. The nurses are unable to please them. This phase is also difficult for the family. The patients direct their anger against their relatives when they are visited by them. It is up to the physician to seek out a dialog with the patient in this phase, and one should not be diverted by a patient's aggressions. It is important for the patient to experience a firmness in the doctor's attitude. The patient must get the impression that nothing can shake the physician—just as nothing can affect the solicitous care of the nurses.

In a third phase (Elisabeth Kübler-Ross, 1973), the patient tries to *bargain and negotiate*, in the hope of obtaining the possibility of living for at least awhile. The individuals concerned think of all the unfulfilled tasks they are leaving, they worry about their spouses, their young children, think about uncompleted professional tasks, about realms of their personality that are still "unlived," about their hunger for life. Religious needs may awaken that until then had remained unstilled. They want to participate in certain events at hand before they die, for example, to take part in the wedding of one of their children. The physician is expected to possess the magic forces to achieve the fulfillment of these wishes, and it is important that the doctor confront the patients during this phase. On the one hand, one does not want to disappoint the patient, but on the other hand, one has to maintain an honest dialog. Most of all, the physician has to show the concerned individual that he or she is available and ready to talk with the relatives and to assist them, if the patient wishes this.

If new operations and emergency surgery become necessary, and with that a new hospital stay, then usually even patients who have denied their ailment with all forces at their disposal—out of a hunger for life and a fear of death—are no longer able to suppress the truth. The feeling of becoming a burden to oneself and to one's family starts to grow in the patient. And the patient has guilt feelings upon realizing that the spouse is suffering too from the long illness. It can no longer be denied that the end of life is imminent. Patients want to review what they fulfilled in life—but also what they failed to achieve, perhaps out of sheer greedy hunger for life. In this phase of *depressive resignation* we cannot simply tell such patients not to become lost in such sad thoughts; they would rightly assume that we are in fact the ones who cannot stand their being depressive. As physicians, we must take it upon us to listen to a patient tell his or her sad thoughts. The patient must have the right to grieve. The patient is at the point of losing all relationships, of having to let go of all objects and activities so dearly loved. We should give the patient the opportunity to express the pain felt. In this phase of the depression, physicians should be able to be with patients without telling them not to be sad. We should be aware that *every* human bound up in such suffering and in the confrontation with death feels to a certain degree alone, since in the end no one can entirely share this last way. Also, in this phase, it is important for the physician not only to care for the patient, but, if the patient allows it, to care for the relatives as well. Often the spouses, parents, or children of such patients cannot stand for their loved ones to be depressed or to hang their head. We have to explain to them and other relatives that this depression is understandable if we remember that this person is being confronted with the fact of soon having to say goodbye to everybody and everything. Grief and desperation are difficult to bear, but only few do not experience these moments. If the family is successful in sharing the process of mourning, it will save the patient from hardship. Patients then feel accepted—in and with their suffering—and do not have the impression of only having been accepted during the good and happy days. Depression is a part of human life, and that in no small measure. Only when the relatives accept their mourning do the terminally ill have at least the impression of a certain common ground. Especially physicians should not take on optimism as a defense mechanism and thus flee their duty as companions in times of most severe anguish.

This is the time in which patients can best exchange profound truths with the physician. But it is also the stage during which the family, if accordingly oriented by the physician, can find a way to the patient. If patients are informed about the nature of the ailment, a more open relationship to their spouses, children, and parents is able to grow than if lies must be sustained until the end.

In a further phase, that of *acceptance*, if the patient lives to experience it and if the patient is able to express his/her feelings with the physician and with family members, he/she mostly does not fight fate. The patient is no longer low-spirited or angry, but rather feels tired and weak, and dozes or sleeps in short intervals: It appears to be the patient's wish to prolong the time of sleeping. As Kübler-Ross (1973) states, in this phase the family usually needs more help than the patient. Patients reach a certain degree of consent with the inevitable; their world becomes ever narrower; they desire to live in peace, do not want to be disturbed any more by news and problems; their hunger for life is extinguished; they concentrate on their attitude toward the inevitable. It makes this last time easier if patients are surrounded by relatives, who take part in their fate, so that they may somehow pass on how and to what purpose they had lived.

❖Starvation

Human beings fear little more than to have to suffer hunger. Regular food supply is vital to us. Even when just a single meal is lacking do we begin to suffer from a tormenting feeling of hunger. Many people eat snacks between meals since they cannot stand the feeling of hunger until the next main meal when their stomach "growls." Apparently, the stomach movements and a secretion of gastric fluids through hunger torment such people. Stunkard and Fox (1971), however, observed in a longitudinal study that gastric and duodenal motility have no effect on the hunger feeling or on the desire for food intake in normal test persons. In a similar study, which lasted only 4 hours and included a larger group of people, the same authors found a strict correlation between gastric motility and the intensity of the hunger feeling only in a small minority of people. As mentioned in an earlier chapter, in later ulcer patients it is their being excessively "tuned" to hunger, their excessive need to incorporate and to take possession of objects which finally lead to an overproduction of pepsinogen and the erosion of the mucous membrane of the stomach.

When people go on a "hunger strike" to "soften up" others, though their suffering is self-chosen, it is certainly no less bothersome. But total emotional concentration on a single goal can apparently force even physiologic needs or pain into the background.

When no food is consumed, after the first few days an increasing hunger ketosis occurs in the blood, and through the lack of fluids and electrolyte compensation, the blood pressure falls and nausea occurs. This state should not be compared to the zero-diet under therapeutic conditions held by obese people, since during such dietary measures the patient is constantly looked after to ensure that the body has enough fluids and the correct concentration of electrolytes.

In longer periods of fasting, the body proteins are also affected and included in the catabolic process. The individual thus lives off not only the energetic reserves (fats), but also the anabolic substances (proteins). In total food deprivation, however, protein catabolism (protein decomposition) is gradually limited to a minimum, so that nitrogen elimination (the nitrogen comes from the catabolized protein molecules) drops to less than 4 g a day after a few weeks. If the protein stock of the organism drops to more than the half the normal amount, a life-threatening state is reached since total protein reserves consist only of 6000 to 8000 g. A fasting regimen of more than 4 months' duration is thus a direct threat to life, even if a reduction of the nitrogen elimination to less than 4 g per day is present. This means, however, that under certain circumstances a human may be able to survive for months without intake of calories (Saudek & Felig, 1976). If the above-mentioned zero-diet is carried out with obese adults, it should not last more than 100 days without maintaining the nitrogen balance. If elimination of ketones through drinking and normal kidney function is provided for during zero-diets, the acid-base balance remains preserved, so that the bothersome nausea can be prevented.

A significant drop in blood sugar concentration results even after a one-day fast (Göschke et al., 1976). Other metabolic changes can be found in the hunger state as well, for example, an increase in pancreas-glucagon concentration in the blood and, in parallel, a fall in plasma insulin. According to Göschke and co-workers (1976), a change in the insulin/glucagon quotient is decisive to the provision of energy-giving substrates during fasting. A totally starving person without the possibility of imbibing the necessary fluids can, if no other intercurrent illnesses are present, survive for up to 30 days.

The experiences in hunger regions of India and in former times in China, in Cambodia and in the Nazi concentration camps show that often a *vita minima* is possible for months or even years under the most precarious food conditions. Those concerned, however, display physically the severe consequences of such chronic hunger. They look totally emaciated because of the extreme loss of weight, and their body tissue has a diminished ability to bind water because of modified protein catabolism. Increased and repeated urination on the one hand, and progressive damage to all organ systems including the central nervous system on the other, are the result. With long-lasting hunger, however, brain metabolism adjusts to the elimination of mainly betaoxybutyric acid and other ketones, which, as mentioned, increase in the blood because of a change in total metabolism to fat combustion. But chronic malnutrition eventually leads to a lack of vitamins, which in turn can lead to very serious damage to the nervous system.

In certain religions, days or even months of fasting are foreseen, whereby "fasting" can mean different things. For some, food is eliminated completely, whereas others are allowed to eat only at night—and adherents of again other religions are allowed to eat only certain foods during this time. The reduction of food or total fasting is meant to further introspection and the recognition of God, and facilitate a relationship with a supernatural, spiritual power. Metaphorically speaking, humans are to free themselves, at least for the time given, of the chains of regular food intake and open themselves to communication with a higher being.

The starvation suffered in the Nazi concentration camps under a constant danger of death are barely imaginable. In 1952, Helweg-Larsen et al. published a comprehensive paper on hunger and starvation in German concentration camps during the Third Reich, and described especially the acute and long-term harm to health incurred. They pointed out that the prisoners lived in a state of lawlessness under dreadful sanitary conditions, and that it was the intention of the guards to break the prisoners' self-respect totally and to expose them—before physical destruction—to complete psychic humiliation and annihilation. The authors mention the completely insufficient diet maintained in these camps with the resulting increased morbidity and mortality. Besides the fact that the average caloric intake was very low, and that malnutrition resulted alone for that reason, the food was of a poor quality. The prisoners suffered extreme weight loss, developed hunger edemas, polyuria and pollacuria since fluids could no longer be retained because of protein catabolism and the body's inability to absorb water. They suffered as well from muscular atrophy as a result of the above-mentioned protein catabolism, very serious avitaminoses, and hunger diarrhea. In addition, because of their weakened general physical state, they were especially prone to infectious diseases.

Hunger and the experience of brutality through the concentration camp guards as well as the constant danger of imminent death led these people to "survive" apathetically. They were unable to think about the past or the future, they lost the ability to have spontaneous reactions, were inclined to irritability and emotional lability. All feelings of pleasure vanished. Yet the suffering of such intense hunger only rarely led to an acute psychotic decompensation.

Hunger was often coupled with a dreadful thirst. Jenö Schwarz (1962) wrote in his book *Mein Kampf auf Leben und Tod* (My life and death struggle) how exhausted he was on his flight from the SS, and how much he missed experiencing human consolation. An SS-man stood on the other side of the river, watching him with binoculars, and from time to time shouted ironically: "Kri, kri, kri." The author described his state as follows:

I sit up and want to start off. But after the first step I fall down again. My head strikes the hard, ice-covered earth. I struggle to my feet because I have to get away from here. But this time too I can only take one step. Again my head strikes the ice because my hands are not able to dampen the impact. They are frozen. Now blood is also flowing from my head. I am forced to stop walking and have to put up with staying here on the ground, waiting for what will come. I feel miserable, so helpless, so deserted. My limbs are shaking from the cold. I have to urinate, but suppress it because I can't even open the button of my trousers. Finally, I no longer can hold it back. Also, a dreadful thirst is torturing me. I lie on my stomach and lick the frozen snow. My hands are no longer able to even bring something to my mouth. My right hand has become totally numb, as if dead. The left one I can still lift, but the fingers are unmovable and stiff.

In his book *Retour d'Auschwitz* (Return from Auschwitz), Guy Kohen (1946) describes the terrible conditions the concentration camp prisoners were exposed to and mentions especially the horrible hunger they had to suffer:

The camp where we were was foreseen for lodging 3000 prisoners. We were perhaps 20,000. In fact, it was nearly bursting from the internees who had come from all the concentration camps of Upper East Silesia (Auschwitz, Monowitz, Janina, Tcherbinia, Jawischowitz, etc.). Under terrible conditions we were packed together like sardines in a tin; at night, we slept in layers, one on top of the other; it was infernal . . . For four days no food was distributed to us . . .

Hermann Adler, who also experienced life in a concentration camp, wrote in his work *Gesänge aus der Stadt des Todes* (Songs from the city of death) (1945) the following about the death trains that entered the concentration camps, and he mentions thereby the torturing experience of thirst:

Only slowly did the trains of horror move on; and during the journey they often stood still for hours on a sidetrack.
The air has long been exhausted, and in the completely closed wagons one is already feverish for water, but no one has the strength to complain.
A few die of suffocation during the ride, expiring while still standing

in the crowded car—and are even envied by some.
The weak and sick, the young and the old, all nearly collapsing,
roll innocently closer to the gas chambers and die before the murderers
desire.

In the aftermath of the war in Indochina, the people of Cambodia experienced sheer unimaginable suffering and hunger. After unutterable suffering millions of people died of starvation. It is immeasurable what these people had to suffer, languishing unnoticed by the world. Again, it was not hostile armies that made them starve, but the ruling minority in the country which made the majority suffer the fate of hunger. People who are starving are so weakened that they cannot draw others' attention to their suffering. So much of the population wasted away without world authorities, such as the United Nations, really turning their attention to the matter.

Throughout history enemies have tried to starve out each other, but only in the 20th century did members of the same society declare others to be "undesirables" and systematically starve them and eradicate them by the millions. The cruel fate of chronic starvation, which today could easily be put to an end through the technical means and production rates at our disposal, was instituted as a means of power and destruction. It has always been dangerous when narcissistically disturbed people were at the helm. With modern possibilities of manipulation, however, it can result in millions of people going hungry and finally dying of starvation.

Here, we have to ask ourselves whether starvation today refers only on the lack of physical nourishment. Do we not all suffer from a "hunger" for basic human solidarity, for the interest of human beings in each other's fate? Do we not all suffer from a "hunger" for human attention in a world that constantly demands more and more adaptation to norms and machines, and that hardly allows one to show any feelings? It is hard to fathom how much pain and suffering people can cause each other. May the time come in which people will consciously renounce the—illusory—feelings of power, cease to cause suffering from hunger, and allow each and every human being again the unburdened pleasure of living.

❖The Hunger for Life

We all, especially when we feel healthy, are always eager to have new experiences. As already mentioned, the human nervous system is constructed such that it needs stimuli in order to retain a healthy functional balance. Besides maternal attention and warmth, the toddler needs constant stimulation through external impulses to develop prosperously. The elderly are often considered as being curious (or even nosey). This is sometimes held against them, although today it is known that people who experience only little are in danger of being directed too much toward their fantasy world. Many states of confusion in the aged might originate not only in an organic brain disease, but also in the fact that they no longer have as many experiences and are thus exposed to a "sensory deprivation"—through which, as is well known, hallucinations can occur, apparently as a substitute for missing impressions of the outer world. But especially youths want to "experience something."

Already in earlier centuries young people travelled to foreign countries and continents. They served in foreign armies and returned happy—as long as they were successful and had managed to stay alive. They reported on their rich and adventurous experiences. The foreign legion and the mercenary armies of the past would not have been possible without this hunger for adventures among young people, especially among those who grew up in disadvantaged emotional and material milieus.

If we consider why riots involving youths have recently occurred especially in rich countries such as Switzerland, Germany and The Netherlands, we do not arrive at a conclusion based on clear scientific inquiries; but we may presume that a saturated social life regulated by computer-based norms frightens young people. Only little individual freedom of decision and of action is left to satisfy their hunger and thirst for inquiry.

The computer and computer software allow us, on the one hand, to collect and to calculate data that in former times not even several human lives could have mastered. Young people entering society today thus get unhoped-for insight into the secrets of nature. On the other hand, this actually removes the mystery from the world. Adolescents and others can no longer project their inner needs onto an unknown "heaven." One of the achievements of the computer age is also the already mentioned standardization of human life. The radius of freedom in everyday life has become smaller. Hardly anyone today can express whims. This span between extreme standardization on one hand, and the unimaginable freedom gained through computer calculations on the other hand, might be one of the causes of insecurity among today's adolescents. We have gained the ability to manipulate the genetic code and to destroy the world with atomic bombs. We have the power over life and death and through this capacity now possess what was earlier attributed to the gods or to God. The narcissistic wound of human vulnerability is compensated for by fantasies of grandiosity. The natural hunger for experience has been taken to gigantic dimensions. Incredible speed and with it the erroneous belief of invulnerability, the human aspiration to advance more and more into the universe, to exploit the moon in the service of man—all of these have become ideas that occupy the normal citizen.

In addition, youths are frightened and wonder whether they will still find a job. Of course, in some countries they can get unemployment compensation, but they may remain dissatisfied. In some cities I have observed how jobless adolescents drive big cars or motorcycles aimlessly and at high speeds through the streets; some of them love to make noise at night because they have nothing to do that might satisfy them. Maybe they are trying, at least unconsciously, to wake up the town's citizens and to make them aware of their misery. They have a hunger for a real commitment to others, but are aware that their entire life energy is going totally unused.

Whether in the East or in the West, these problems of youth have not yet been solved. Neither the manipulation of the masses in the East nor capitalistic life in the West, bare of solidarity among those who live there, can help these young people in their hunger for life. A new division into population classes is impending: The first is composed of people who take part in the achievements of computer technology, the second of those who only have auxiliary functions in this society, and the third, as can already be seen today, of those who do not even have the possibility to work, but who get a kind of pension through their unemployment compensation. Such an existence without goals and the possibility for engaging in society is usually experienced as being senseless. Those responsible—and who does not belong to this group?—will have to come up with better ideas than to date to

118

help develop the solidarity in society that mediates to all the true impression of participating in the increase of human knowledge—the expansion of "the clearing of existence," as the existential analysts say—and in the furtherance of every citizen.

In order to reach the goal of satisfying youths' hunger for life, at least to a certain degree, it will also be necessary to change our school system. Not only, as the author has mentioned elsewhere (Battegay, 1972), will it be necessary to create regular group-centered possibilities in schools to work through and to settle conflicts, but also more so than presently the case the regular lessons will have to be led in a group-centered manner. Teachers should be urged to let the pupils, through their counseling, teach themselves by repeatedly allowing them to assume responsibility, and by letting them contribute to the lessons. It should also be considered whether the pupils in such group-centered classes are able to grade themselves. The old grading system would be obsolete, and the pupils would develop a feeling—a sensibility—for whether they are capable or not of following a higher educational program. Of course, supervision by an expert—though not in an authoritarian manner—would have to be present. The hunger of young people for assuming responsibility would thus be satisfied to a certain degree, and their actual readiness for assuming such responsibility would be furthered. Often civil studies are demanded; but theoretical instruction in civil duties would be counterproductive. Yet such a "responsibility training," as explained above, could motivate today's youth to assume their civil duties in the future.

With their hunger for action, youths today have in several respects more difficulties than former generations. On the one hand, the population is growing ever older; on the other hand, it takes longer today to become fully integrated into professional and social life. When does one's youth end? Upon reaching majority, be it at 18 or 20 years, adolescents often have not yet reached a position in society in which they are considered fully equal to those who have a clear professional status. One's income and professional position often decide whether an individual is taken seriously or not in decision processes. In many respects, the time of youth has even been expanded up to the 30th year of life. Modern society has strict regulations, yet it gives young people neither a responsible role nor social status: They are expected to learn, but not to join in the discussion on solving problems—though in no other phase of life is the personal need to take a decisive role greater than in one's younger years. For some older people today, even a 50-year-old may still be held to be "young"!

Although physical and intellectual maturation proceeds more quickly now than some decades ago (acceleration), emotional development is often delayed (retardation). People are not seldom affectively infantile and behave regressively up to an advanced age because their sense of responsibility was not properly trained. Infantilism may even have become a positive cultural phenomenon in our time. Which elderly person now wants to look old? They wish to give the impression of being youthful up to old age and behave like young men and women. Retaining unrestrained youthfulness throughout one's lifetime has become one of the most popular ideologies of our century.

The hunger for life of young people is essentially a healthy phenomenon. It is nothing new that the stormy youths on the one hand and the guardians of tradition on the other hand enter into a conflict of generations. Perhaps today's generation of adults, however, is the first one that appears to be surprised by this phenomenon: They want the young to join in completely in the computer-normed clockwork, accepting unexamined and uncritically, for example, the dominance of performance and competition in professional life and leisure time, constant economic growth and the necessity of the utilization of nuclear power as embodiments of true wisdom. Obviously, these are expectations that especially those young people cannot fulfill who did not have the opportunity to experience a primal confidence in their familiar surroundings during early and later childhood (Erikson, 1950) in a supportive community that would have given them a life-long feeling of security. Not the happy ones are heading for the streets to destroy shop windows or take drugs, but those who have become ill and full of existential doubt because of a lack of or an overabundance of protection, or parental attention only on the condition of "ideal" behavior during childhood. These are the ones we must especially take care of. We should not project all of society's failure on them. Ways and means have to be found to integrate them into an environment in which they feel more or less sheltered. Autonomous youth centers can never solve the problem alone, since they tend to become ghettos. The general public must learn to feel more solidarity with these young people. Only in this way can these people—for whom entry into the modern world is difficult—find a place where they can experience their existence as something significant.

In London, Hyde Park Corner has existed for a long time as a place where people are allowed to speak freely, and where anyone can listen who likes to. Also, musicians playing string or wind instruments can be seen traveling through the towns of continental Europe, and many people stop and listen with great interest. This is the beginning of a development that could result in many places in our cities becoming meeting points where speakers, musicians, and listeners can become a community and develop a sense of mutuality.

The hunger of young people for action and human attention should not be repressed: It is the very thing that keeps mankind going. Our cities must maintain enough hospitality that the young people are not left to themselves and become estranged from the world. They should be allowed to experience, and to express, their hunger in every sense—but also to have the impression that others are willing to try to understand their feelings.

❖Insatiability in Politics and the "Indigestibility" of the Conquest

From the past as well as the present we know that in dictatorships there are always men in leading positions who are driven by an excessive eagerness to gain personal importance. Through their subordinates they try to compensate their feelings of insufficiency and their communication difficulties, which more or less always originate in experiences of deficiency concerning love, attention, and stimulation in their early childhood—be it from a genetically determined insensibility or a failure in the environment. Their narcissistic needs result from a deficient development of an adequate self and realistic object representation. Their "hunger" for being recognized, stimulated, and approved of is insatiable.

Such "hungry" people, damaged in their self (Kohut, 1971, 1977, Battegay, 1977), may climb very high on the social and political ladder, since their tendency to compensate their deficient self gives them the motivation to remove all obstacles to their career. They use their intelligence preponderantly in the service of their ambitions. The realization of their compensating fantasies of grandiosity results in the end in a leading position. There is, however, the danger that, with proper ideological support, they will soon start making despotic demands of the people for what they themselves need in their fantasy to fill up their "narcissistic hole" (Ammon, 1974). Their subordinates are expected to do or undo what the ideology or fantasy of these narcissistically deficient people demands. These people have a "hunger" for power, and they will use all means to take possession of and to incorporate objects with which they unconsciously try to reinforce their own selves. If such a "statesman" speaks in the name of his people (but without asking them), he feels reinforced by the sheer millions of individuals in "his" nation. Without democratic control such persons can become very dangerous, because everybody and everything standing in the way are experienced as hindrances, causing offence and danger. There are hardly more pronounced despotic systems than those ruled by such narcissistically disturbed leaders. Of course, it is not by chance that the narcissistically deficient members of the leading class of a political system that takes its ideology to be absolute always applaud each other. The pretentious and uncritical applause of all for one and of this person for himself and for the others is obviously meant to mutually reinforce their weak self-esteem.

It is dangerous to restrict parliamentary control. In an autocratically ruled system, people who are "hungry" for power will inevitably make their way to the top. The constant growth of the narcissistic hunger of such people is unavoidable. The urge to take possession of and to incorporate objects leads to ever more "swallowing" of objects, since as soon as an object is possessed and incorporated, it can no longer be experienced as such because it has now stopped to exist as a separate entity: An irresistible and insatiable desire for objects results which is characteristic of addictions.

Apparently to the amazement of the democratic countries, Hitler, after having finalized the Munich Convention with them in 1938, was still "hungry" to take possession of and to incorporate more and more countries into the German "Reich." Undoubtedly, he was from childhood on most severely disturbed in his ego functions and in his narcissism, and therefore replete with feelings of insufficiency he could not bear without compensation. Thus, he tried to reinforce his self, as it were, with the help of the German people. When speaking in the Sportpalast in Berlin or elsewhere, in his fantasy he entered into a fusion at least with those present, though certainly with all other Germans, too. The projective establishment of enemies, on the inside as well as on the outside, helped him to harbor his own aggressions and the respective compensatory fantasies of grandiosity concerning his own racial "mission" and that of all German culture. But because his fragmentation-prone ego and his tendency toward projective identifications (projecting his own aggressivity onto others) could never disappear and his "narcissistic hole" never be "filled up" lastingly, his "hunger" necessarily remained unsatiated. The repeated applause of his own people did not satisfy him; rather, he impulsively conquered one adjoining country after the other until at last he attacked Russia, thereby misjudging his own power and that of Germany according to his compensatory delusion of the German "superman." The broad, world-wide dimension of the Allied forces and of the Russians, as well as the climatic conditions in Eastern Europe, were his doom. In his unsatiated hunger for more and more countries, he was trying to incorporate a piece that both he and Germany were not able to "swallow" and to take possession of. No political power on earth can go beyond the dimensions corresponding to the possibilities of its citizens concerning organizational capabilities and human resources. A dictatorship carries with it, through its insatiability based on the narcissistic disorder of its leaders, the very seed of its own ruin.

Characteristic of Hitler's severe ego pathology and his concomitant narcissistic disturbance were his impulse breakthroughs, his tendency toward rage and fury, his tendency to divide the world into good and bad objects, his extreme narcissistic vulnerability, and his way of thinking that reminds one of the primary process of the unconscious—all typical for borderline personalities. Hitler, who was easily insulted and hurt by mere trifles, did his utmost to triumph over others or to eliminate those he considered bad. In their never-ending history of subjugation since biblical times, the Jews' very existence reminded him, in his profoundly felt narcissistic insufficiency, of his own impotence. This might be an explanation for his hope of being revalorized through projective identification, i.e., by projecting his own aggressivity onto the Jews and by murdering them in the "final solution." The very severe disturbance in his self caused him to enter into a fusion in his fantasy with similarly thinking people. Thus did he gather his National Socialist followers around him, people who were similarly disturbed and therefore ready to let themselves be used for his ideology. They corrupted their superego by raising their ideology to an ego-ideal: They believed they were on a higher level of existence. How fast a whole nation, many members of which felt resentful because of the defeat in World War I and the subsequent high unemployment, can be seized by a compensatory fantasy of a "superman"—even in the 20th century—becomes evident in this example of Germany. Such a movement of narcissistically deficient people replete with feelings of revenge can be stopped only in a solid democracy with a secure parliamentary system.

Wherever a tradition and/or training of the citizens in democratic rules and functions is missing, such marginal groups of revengeful, power-hungry, narcissistically deficient people who sell themselves to an ideology to enhance their self-esteem can suddenly become dominant and motivate the whole people and/or subjugate it.

In revolutionary processes as well we often see narcissistically "hungry" people in leading positions. Individuals tend to take part in revolutions who cannot accept any delay in the realization of their "high" ideals and aims. The entire world should accept their ideas and ideologies regardless of the real conditions. Such individuals either will be disappointed later on if the revolution becomes reality since this reality will necessarily differ from their expectations and their need for a narcissistic fusion; or they will try more and more radically to change reality according to their own design.

A revolution, it is said, devours its own children because the new and insatiable followers of a demanding, odd ideology experience even those as "not belonging" who once represented them in leading positions. Besides the fact that a learning process takes place during a revolution with respect to aggressions, such an explosive political process contains the danger of unrealistic expectations and thus of great disappointments—which once again must be overcome aggressively. Ideology wants to subdue reality instead of taking social reality into account.

Each society, each nation ought to see to it that narcissistically insatiable persons are kept away from the seats of power. A humane and fair society can exist only if insatiability is restrained. Everyone must realize that political power, which maintains itself at the expense of the submission of other people or other nations, cannot endure. A political structure that is the result of such an insatiable attempt to take over and maintain power cannot be held together permanently, even with very strict laws and massive threats and actions of a secret police. Those who cannot restrict their hunger for power contribute to their own and to their state's downfall.

Interesting in this context is the "hunger strike" of prisoners who had unconditionally joined a terrorist group. They apparently want to force their fellow citizens to have pity with those who threatened them in their lives before imprisonment. People who resort to a "hunger strike" always want to show the surrounding world their own power by directing guilt onto others. Through a "hunger strike" such "hungry" people thus succeed in making their surroundings suffer. Maybe a "hunger strike" is also a reminder of the fact that the people concerned did not succeed in satisfying their "hunger" for power in another way.

Mahatma Gandhi had an enormous power in India with his hunger strikes. His going hungry also represented, pars pro toto, the suffering of his people. The colonial power knew that if anything happened to him during the hunger strikes, the whole nation would revolt.

Maybe the hunger strike also represents insatiability. Small concessions do not satisfy the individual on a hunger strike. He or she wants a total breakthrough, the "total object," as Melanie Klein (1935) would say. The resulting danger is that satisfaction is not obtained even when the desired aim is reached. Reality usually differs from the image an ideology purports. However, for people in countries ruled by dictators, there is sometimes nothing else left than going on a hunger strike if they want to stage an effective fight against the abuse of power.

❖Epilogue

It is today probably a common human problem not to feel sufficiently embedded in one's environment. Many people, especially with our cultural background, suffer from the feeling of not getting enough human warmth and recognition. Here, we must consider that, contrary to other primates, Homo sapiens enters the world, as Portmann (1944) says, prematurely and thus still is in need of a "social uterus" for proper development. The infant cannot even regulate its own warmth. After having experienced the body-warm milieu intra utero, the newborn enters a cool and inhospitable world. If, in the first months of life, one does not experience in the environment the warmth, stimulation, and Gestalt cognition possibilities that are essential to development, this will have an effect on one's entire life. Indeed, for these reasons, all human beings of our cultural milieu have been "shorted" on warmth and loving care, since it is never again possible for them to experience such a warm, secure feeling as they did in the womb. The trauma of birth (Rank, 1924) leads us out of the realm of almost absolute protection into the draft of a demanding world. The newborn's cry shows what the small child aggressively demands—not only nourishment, but also warm care. To a certain degree, all human beings who grow up in our cultural surroundings are impaired in their experience of self-value because they never received full compensation for this birth trauma. In their early childhood they all suffered a certain deficit of warmth and loving care. Self- and object representations grow within them that also always bear the signs of insufficiency. This deficiency in self- and object representation, the lack of experiences of self-value, and the insufficient estimation of objects are the reasons motivating them throughout life to obtain a better self and a more complete object. However, those who, in the author's point of view, suffer from a hunger disease are especially, and in a specific way, damaged in their experience of self- and object value. They therefore insatiably chase after objects their whole life long in order to undergo a fusion with them so as to enhance and reinforce their own selves—and to understand just what an object is. These individuals have the tendency to take total possession of persons close to them or of a broader environment; or if they experienced overprotection, temptations, or misidentifications on the part of their parents, they tend to reject strictly every offer of an object and to draw the world's attention through their suffering. The insatiable incorporation and taking possession of objects by the obese, by bulimics, by persons addicted to alcohol, prescribed medicines, or drugs, and the respective tendency in depressives, as well as the complete rejection of objects by patients with anorexia nervosa, culminating in a masochistic triumph, are all evidence of the inability of these people to experience mature object relationships. They are fixated to that early childhood experience where there was no control over object hunger, and where circumstances easily occurred in which every object was incorporated and taken possession of, or was rejected totally for a shorter or a longer time. Human beings who lived their early childhood in a deficient milieu or who were not able to experience the warm care offered and who hardly had the possibility of constructing a self- and object representation in their fantasy have the tendency to subject objects under all circumstances, and if this object tries to separate itself from them, to destroy it. They have only few relationships and bonds, and if they succeed in winning over individuals, they do not give them the freedom to detach themselves. In extreme cases, they even murder the person close to them, because they cannot bear them breaking away. The German proverb: "If you don't want to be my brother, then I shall crack your skull" (Willst du nicht mein Bruder sein, so schlag' ich dir den Schädel ein) is true of these individuals. Being people who often suffer terribly from their loneliness and their disturbance of communication, they kill those who, at least temporarily, were once their companions.

Yet everyone has a "hunger" for contact with others. Human relationships are unthinkable without a certain self-love that is extended to the other person during an encounter. The basic human relationship takes place on the basis of the extension of the narcissistic interest (or libido) to the object. This tendency toward fusion in the fantasy should, however, not go so far that the one becomes dependent on the other or both on each other. Otherwise, a pathological tendency develops, with the unconscious aim of reinforcing one's self by total inclusion of others into one's own world and narcissism. Individuals who are especially "hungry" for human contact usually suffer from a narcissistic deficit—a lack in their self with a corresponding deficiency in their experience of self-value. They try to compensate this deficit by the above-mentioned, more or less total inclusion of others in their lives. But also people who have no possibility to transfer their narcissistic attention to others, and who cannot give some of their self-love to others because they only have little left for themselves, should be considered ill. Although they are deeply in need of human contact, they are—mostly because of ego weakness or a fragmentation tendency of their ego—completely unable to turn their "hunger" for human relationships into reality. Such individuals live "autistically" by themselves (although they would prefer to live very differently), mostly because they feel they are too vulnerable when faced with the outside world. They perceive themselves as defenseless, at the mercy of the surroundings, and as unable to delineate themselves sufficiently from other human beings.

In a depression, regardless of its origin, there is always a narcissistic depletion, a more or less total absence of the experience of self-value. The essence of depression lies in this disturbance within the narcissistic realm, in the dearth of narcissistic information available to the ego, which normally gives us not only the impression of own value, but also that of belonging. Whether for more or less apparent genetic reasons, from a brain disorder, from other physical causes or because of early childhood conditions or more recent life events, depression is always determined by the lack of or dwindling of this central self-representation or ability to consider the psychic instances of Id, Ego, Superego (in other words, the whole psychodynamics) as belonging to oneself. It has to be presumed that the disturbances of the transmitter metabolism in the brains of depressive people is linked closely with this narcissistic deficiency. Those suffering from depressions deeply long for human contact, although they often avoid every form of communication. Inside, they expect others to break through the barrier, to approach them, and to recognize their need. Depressives always have huge expectations of objects. It is this enormous demand that is at the center of depression, because inevitably it will be disappointed by human surroundings. Even in the major (endogenous) depressive disorders there are corresponding release dynamics. Indeed, such people have a genetic tendency toward depressions (which reveals itself also in their heredity), but the decisive factors are often disappointments concerning closely related persons which result nearly automatically from their excessive expectations of these objects.

In their insatiability, addicts are the prototypes of people suffering from a hunger disease: They struggle for compensation for an early experience of deficiency regarding love and stimulation by incorporating and taking possession of objects. The loving care of close persons is not enough for them. Rather, they try again and again to cling to objects, to take possession of them and/or to swallow them. If they succeed in getting hold of or incorporating the objects they desired, the object value of these objects, which have now become part of them, disappears. The French proverb says: "To embrace it is to lose it" ("Tout embrasser c'est tout perdre"). It is common knowledge that those who want everything lose everything. This fact results not only because humans will never be able to comprehend immeasurable things, but also because one cannot estimate the true value of objects when the tendency reigns to incorporate or to take total possession thereof—when they have become parts of us. One is still hungry and still struggles insatiably for objects. Up to a certain point, this "addictive" view of the world characterizes all human beings, especially those of our cultural background. We constantly struggle to obtain new stimuli and objects to assist us in our self-fulfillment—and yet no sooner have we gained them do we lose all interest in them because they have become a part of ourselves; or as we say, they have become our possession. But what we own, we often barely notice. We are insatiably on the lookout for new objects. It is sufficiently well known today in partnerships between men and women as well as in other kinds of pairs that one usually looks around for other partners who are presumed to be even more stimulating to us. Indeed, this fact is the reason that we become hungry again for other objects once we are sure of an object—and remain insatiable. It is human insatiability that brings so much suffering into human relationships. The same insatiable tendency causes a continual struggle in humans for ever new possessions and new power, and has above all a disastrous effect in politics. The insatiability of human beings—their hunger for power—may even cause them to employ weapons that could in the end lead to the complete destruction of mankind. This tendency, present in all modern societies, needs to be brought under control. The United Nations Organization has so far often turned out to be merely a site of ideological warfare, of hunger for power, of insatiable ambitions. We have at least a temporary reprieve, as these battles are presently being held only verbally. Yet over and over again, bloody armed conflicts

132

break out. Nations are attacked, especially by political systems who claim to be fighters for a higher cause. And for the sake of an ideology (in reality: for power reasons) human beings are imprisoned, massacred, slaughtered, terror organizations are furthered, neighboring states or even groups from one's own people are attacked or poisoned. The whole world should see how far a dictator's and a dictatorship's sphere of influence reaches. Revenge is sworn without end, and the expansion of one's own domain is meant. This dangerous game can end disastrously if the hunger for power behind it is not recognized as such, limited, channelled, and socially controlled. Yet we should not construct a "hunger" taboo; that would be the wrong way. Rather, it is necessary to use this insatiable hunger and the respective aggressiveness for activities that bring together and bind.

We no longer need long work days because the computer is replacing humans in many areas. Everybody could in fact lead a quiet and peaceful life. But in many places there is still a hunger for work or even a work mania. Both could be applied to social activities. The old social classes based on socioeconomic conditions are disappearing; the industrial worker no longer belongs to the "proletariat." The modern worker takes part in technological achievements and the resulting prosperity. New classes are now appearing, arising from the fact that some take part in the world of computers, whereas others are only able to carry out auxiliary functions, a third group having no possibility to work at all. Although in the countries of our cultural background social services today fill this gap and thus guarantee everyone their daily bread, those who are not allowed to experience the joy of being productive are frustrated and feel they are being put aside. Their hunger to be meaningfully occupied and active finds no satisfaction, no reward. It is not enough to have welfare institutions available for everybody. Though much has already been achieved in that no one has to go hungry physically, those who do not feel themselves to be active, participating parts of our social system will remain "hungry" for approval of work well done. Here, a sense of solidarity among human beings must be developed which goes far beyond what is commonly experienced. We are all "sitting in the same boat" and cannot simply say that the fate of others is of no interest to us. Pollution alone and the extreme endangerment through modern weapons systems prove that no one can declare that acting this way or that is a private matter or the matter of a single group. In a story in the Talmud, several people are sitting in a boat, when suddenly one of them starts to dig a hole under his seat. Asked what he is doing, he answers that he is digging this hole only under his own seat. Obviously, all people on the boat would drown together. Today's technical possibilities and the dimensions of potential construction and destruction challenge us to recognize our desire for life, our thirst for action as well as our greed for power and to use them, properly transformed, for the good of all.

Of course, hunger is also the result of the body's natural metabolism. If we are healthy, we awake each morning hungry, and yet once satisfied, we again develop a feeling of hunger after some time. The metabolism of diabetics is similar in many respects to that of hunger. This state of the metabolism, however, cannot be changed simply by supplying food, because the impaired metabolism prevents or impedes adjustment. The respective medical measures or substances see to it that these people survive this "hunger disease." But these people also need the positive emotional support of the doctor, who confirms them in their self-value and gives them courage, which adds essentially to a pleasurably experienced life. Also, certain gastrointestinal disturbances such as stomach or duodenal ulcers can be considered (at least partly) as expressions of an unsatiated or insatiable hunger. The stomach of such people, particularly their secretion of pepsinogen, indicates that they are constantly "hungry." Besides the medicinal restraint of the secretion of gastric juices or other medical measures, these individuals need the attention of the doctor, not limited to a strictly objective appraisal, but also giving the patients the feeling of not (or at least not completely) having to be disappointed in their—still relatively extreme—expectations toward others. The doctor ought to give patients confidence by listening to them and recognizing their innermost emotions—even if not all their wishes for being cared for can be fulfilled.

Especially heart and circulatory ailments, above all coronary diseases, reveal that often individuals are concerned who have developed an insatiable hunger for action and high ambitions. They demand much of themselves and flee any resulting disappointments and depressive moods, thus satisfying at least some of their expectations. Those type-A individuals who, according to Rosenman et al. (1975/1976) and Friedman and Rosenman (1974), never rest because they want or have to "devour" everything aggressively (for their own self-approval) are in danger of eventually falling prey to a heart or circulatory disease and, if they do not adjust their life patterns correspondingly, of dying from this. In people suffering from essential hypertension, the fact that their "hunger" for action is often inhibited leads to further tensions.

Yet, in all of the above-mentioned hunger diseases the question of how it came to the "chosen organ or organ system" is unresolved. A definitive answer is to date not available. Doubtlessly, genetic and environmental factors (in the case of gastro-duodenal ulcers and infections) are co-responsible, without certainty as to which ones specifically contributed what. In certain hunger diseases, for example, anorexia nervosa, the course of the disease can also be considered from the vantage point of the aims inherent to it. The (unconsciously) displayed "hunger" of anorectics is meant to drastically show the environment how much they have missed loving care in their childhood and later on, right up to the present day.

When one speaks of "hunger," one also means the fact that human beings today have become more demanding perhaps because no object "fits" them any more. One recalls in this context the story by Franz Kafka (1935) entitled "Ein Hungerkünstler" (A Hunger Artist). When asked by the guard: "Hey, why weren't you able to act otherwise?," he answers: "Because I couldn't find any food I like. If I had found some, believe me, I would have kept quiet and eaten my fill like yourself and everyone else."

The many stimuli we supply ourselves have spoiled us. For many people today nothing has the power of revelation, no longer do objects have the originality they expect and demand. Once they have taken possession of an object or have incorporated it, they ask themselves over and again: "Was that all?" because they missed the object character of the objects as soon as they obtained them. In his novel *Enttäuschung* (Disappointment) Thomas Mann (1951) lets a man be disappointed by all objects—even death will not be what he expects. "... Oh, I already know death so well, the last disappointment! So this is death, I'll say to myself in my last moment, now I am experiencing it! But what is it really?"

When in danger of losing one's life, it may often come to mind how much we have missed out on, and a hunger may ensue to experience as much as possible in the time left. When people afflicted by a serious illness realize their situation, they often fight their fate because they still feel deeply very "hungry" for experiences. It is an even more difficult and cruel destiny if someone has to remain physically or emotionally hungry. The experiences in the concentration camps of the Nazis and elsewhere in which guards torture prisoners in unimaginable ways in the name of a sadistically reigning class, show how morbidity and mortality increase through chronic hunger. If the hunger lasts long, thoughts are restricted to the most essential functions, and the past as well as the future appear unreachable. The hunger for life so typical of humans also slowly declines when one suffers starvation over a long period time. In hunger states one is deprived of one's most essential possession: the desire for life and pleasure. A pleasureable feeling of hunger is noticeable only as long as no hunger disease reigns. When pleasurable hunger cannot be felt, this is evidence that the person is impaired in the central core of life.

Individuals who did not have to suffer physical hunger but are hunger sick because of their growing up under unfavorable conditions which left them empty emotionally and cognitively will have to come to realize, in part on their own, in part through psychotherapeutic assistance, that they are the ones who are best able to reinforce themselves by constantly taking a positive look at the given situations. People who are severely damaged because of their hunger disease have to be helped by the personal engagement of physicians and psychotherapists—but also by their fellow human beings—to overcome anew their doubts and to be convinced of the unwavering human solidarity of the helpers.

❖References

Abraham, K. (1916). Untersuchungen über die früheste prägenitale Entwicklungsstufe der Libido. Internat. Z. ärztliche Psychoanalyse, IV, 2, 7. In K. Abraham (1969). *Psychoanalytische Studien zur Charakterbildung und andere Schriften*. Cremerius J. (Ed.). Frankfurt a.M.: S. Fischer.

Abraham, K. (1924). Versuch einer Entwicklungsgeschichte der Libido auf Grund der Psychoanalyse seelischer Störungen. In: *Neue Arbeiten zur ärztlichen Psychoanalyse, Heft II*, Int. Psychoanalyt. Verlag, und in: *Psychoanalytische Studien zur Charakterbildung und andere Schriften*, p. 3, Conditio Humana, Frankfurt a.M.: S. Fischer, 1969.

Adler, H. (1945). *Gesänge aus der Stadt des Todes*. Zurich/New York: Oprecht.

Alexander, F. (1950). *Psychosomatic medicine*. Berlin/New York: Walter de Gruyter.

Ammon, G. (1974). *Psychoanalyse und Psychosomatik*. München: Piper.

Anand, B. K., & Brobeck, J. R. (1951). Localization of a "feeding center" in the hypothalamus of the rat. *Proc. Soc. Exp. Bio. Med. 77*, 323. In J. R. Brobeck (Ed.) (1979), *Best & Taylor's physiological basis of medical practice* (10th ed.). Baltimore: Williams & Wilkins.

Anand, B. K., & Brobeck, J. R. (1951). Hypothalamic control of food intake in rats and cats. *Yale J. Bio. Med., 24*, 23. In J. R. Brobeck (Ed.) (1979), *Best & Taylor's physiological basis of medical practice* (10th ed.). Baltimore: Williams & Wilkins.

Bachofner, I. M., & Stransky, M. (1977). Erfahrungen in einer Gruppe von Übergewichtigen. *Sozial und Präv. Med., 22*, 139–141.

Battegay, R. (1960). Psychodynamische Verhältnisse bei der Gruppenpsychotherapie. *Psychiat. Neurol. Neurochir., 63*, 333–342.

Battegay, R. (1972). *Der Mensch in der Gruppe. Bd. III* (3rd ed., 1979). Bern/Stuttgart/Wien: Huber.

Battegay, R. (1977). *Narzissmus und Objektbeziehungen* (2nd ed., 1979). Bern/Stuttgart/Wien: Huber.

Battegay, R. (1979). Die ärztliche Aufklärungspflicht, am Beispiel von Schwerkranken. *Schweiz Ärztez., 26*, 219.

Battegay, R. (1981). Totale Fusion mit einem Objekt und dessen Zerstörung. *Schw. Arch. Neurol. Neurochir. Psychiatr., 219*, 283.

Battegay, R. (1981). *Grenzsituationen*. Bern/Stuttgart/Wien: Hans Huber.

Battegay, R. (1986). *Depression* (2nd ed., 1987). Bern/Stuttgart/Wien: Hans Huber.

Battegay, R., Rauchfleisch, U., & Graf von Schliefen, H. (1972). Sozioökonomische Determinanten der Inanspruchnahme der Psychiatrischen Universitätspoliklinik Basel. *Schw. Arch. Neurol. Neurochir. Psychiatr., 111*, 67.

Battegay, R., Lipp, H., Miest, U., Glauser C., & Rauchfleisch, U. (1981). Gruppenpsychotherapie mit Adipösen. *Gruppenpsychotherapie und Gruppendynamik, 7*, 63.

Benedetti, I. G. (1976). *Der Geisteskranke als Mitmensch*. Göttingen: Vandenhoeck & Ruprecht.

Binswanger, I. C., & Herrmann, M. (1979). Psychosomatische Aspekte des Diabetes Mellitus. In Th. von Uexküll (Hrsg.), *Lehrbuch der Psychosomatischen Medizin* (p. 668). München/Wien/Baltimore: Urban & Schwarzenberg.

Bleuler, M. (1952). "Psychosomatik" der Fettsucht. *Helvetica Med. Acta, 19*, 2193.

Bleuler, M. (1954). *Endokrinologische Psychiatrie*. Stuttgart: Thieme.

Bowlby, J. (1973). *Separation. Anxiety and anger. Vol. II: Attachment and loss*. The Hogarth Press and the Institute of Psycho-Analysis.

Brand, J., & Gensicke, P. (1980). Ein verhaltenstherapeutisch-kommunikationstheoretisches Konzept zur stationären Behandlung der Anorexia nervosa. Erste Ergebnisse. *Arch. Psychiat. Nervenkr. 229*, 113–126.

Bray, G. A. (1980). Jejunoileal bypass, jaw wiring, and vagotomy for massive obesity. In A. J. Stunkard (Ed.), *Obesity* (p. 369). Philadelphia/London/Toronto: W. B. Saunders.

Brisman, J., & Siegel, M. (1985). The bulimia workshop: A unique integration of group treatment approaches. *Int. J. Group Psychother., 35*, 585–601.

Brobeck, J. R. (1979). *Best & Taylor's physiological basis of medical practice* (10th ed.). Baltimore: Williams & Wilkins.

Brobeck, J. R., Tepperman, J., & Long, C. N. H. (1943). Experimental hypothalamic hyperphagia in the albino rat. *Yale J. Biol. Med. 5*, 83. Cited in J. R. Brobeck (Ed.) (1979), *Best & Taylor's physiological basis of medical practice* (10th ed.). Baltimore: Williams & Wilkins.

Brotman, A. W., Herzog, D. B., & Hamburg, P. (1988). Long-term course in four bulimic patients treated with psychotherapy. *J. Clin. Psychiatry, 419*(4), 5760.

Bruch, H. (1978). *The Golden cage; The enigma of anorexia nervosa*. Cambridge, MA: Harvard University Press.

Bühler, F. R., Burkart, F., Lütold, B. E., Küng, M., Marbet, G., & Pfisterer, M. (1975). Antihypertensive betablocking action as related to renin and age: A pharmacologic tool to identify pathogenetic mechanisms in essential hypertension. *Amer. J. Cardio., 36*, 635.

Ciompi, L., & Eisert, M. (1971). Etudes catamnestiques de longue durée sur le vieillissement des alcooliques. *Social Psychiatry, 6*(3), 219.

Cohn, C., & Joseph, D. (1962). Influence of body weight and body fat on appetite of "normal" lean and obese rats. *Yale J. Biol. Med., 34*, 5198. Cited in J. R. Brobeck (Ed.) (1979), *Best & Taylor's physiological basis of medical practice* (10th ed.). Baltimore: Williams & Wilkins.

de Poret, D., Pouliquen, A., Dejours, C., & Assan, R. (1984). *Une approche pédagogique globale des diabétiques insulinodépendants*. Unpublished. Département de Diabétologie, Hôpital Bichat, Paris.

Dorfman, W., Slater, S., & Gottlieb, N. (1959). Drug and placebo in group treatment of obesity. *Int. J. Group Psychother., 19*, 345–351.

138

Dunbar, F. H. et al. (1936). The psychic component of the disease process (including convalescence) in cardiac, diabetic and fracture patients. *Am. J. of Psychiatry, 193*, 649–679.

Eitinger, L. (1969). Psychosomatic problems in concentration camp survivors. *J. of Psychosomatic Research, 3*, 83–89.

Eitinger, L. (1969). Rehabilitation of concentration camp survivors (following concentration camp trauma). *Psychother. Psychosom., 7*, 42–49.

Eitinger, L., Krell, R., & Rieck, M. (Eds.) (1985). *The psychological and medical effects of concentration camps and related persecutions on survivors of the Holocaust*. Vancouver: University of British Columbia Press.

Engelhardt, U. (1979). *Leistungsmotiviation und Narzissmus bei orthostatischen Kreislaufstörungen*. Bern, Stuttgart, Wien: Hans Huber.

Erikson, E. H. (1950). *Childhood and society*. New York: Norton.

Fenichel, O. (1946). *The psychoanalytic theory of neurosis*. London: Routhledge & Kegan.

Ferguson, J. M. (1975). *Learning to eat. Behavior modification for weight control*. Palo Alto: Bull.

Freud, S. (1955). *Beyond the pleasure principle. Standard Ed., XVIII*, 764, London: Hogarth Press.

Freud, S. (1957). *Mourning and melancholia. Standard Ed., XIV*, 237–258, London: Hogarth Press.

Freud, S. (1960). *The psychopathology of everyday life. Standard Ed., VI*. London: Hogarth Press.

Freud, S. (1961). *Introductory lectures on psychoanalysis, parts I and II* (195–197). *Standard Ed., XV*. London: Hogarth Press.

Freud, S. (1963). *Introductory lectures on psychoanalysis, part III* (196–197). *Standard Ed., XVI*. London: Hogarth Press.

Freyberger, H., & Strube, K. (1963). Zur Psychodynamik und Psychotherapie gesteigerter Eßbedürftigkeit bei Fettsuchtkranken. *Schweiz. Med. Wschr., 193*, 559.

Friedman, M., & Rosenman, R. H. (1974). *Type A behavior and your heart*. New York: Alfred A. Knopf. Cited in J. P. Henry & P. M. Stephens (Eds.), *Stress health, and the social environment. A sociobiologic approach to medicine*. New York, Heidelberg, Berlin: Springer-Verlag.

Fromm, E. (1973). *The anatomy of human destructiveness*. New York, Chicago, San Francisco: Holt, Rinehart & Winston.

Gellhorn, E., & Loofborrow, G. N. (1963). *Emotions and emotional disorders*. New York, Evanston, London: Hoeber Medical Division, Harper & Row.

Gerlinghoff, M., & Backmund, H. (1987). Stehlen bei Anorexia nervosa und Bulimia nervosa. *Fortschr. Neurol. Psychiat., 55*, 343–346.

Gfeller, R., & Assal, J. Ph. (1979). *Das Krankheitserlebnis des Diabetespatienten. Folia psychopractica 10*. Basel: Hoffman La Roche.

Gfeller, R, & Assal, J. Ph. (1981). Diabetes, ein neues therapeutisches Konzept aus klinisch-diabetologischer sowie medizin-psychologischer Sicht, angewandt an der Diabetes-Station des Genfer Kantonsspitals. *Ther. Umschau, 37*, 43.

Göschke, H., Girard, J., & Stahl, M. (1976). Der Stoffwechsel bei vollständigem Fasten. Unterschiedliches Verhalten bei Männern und Frauen sowie bei Normalpersonen und Adipösen. *Klin. Wschr., 54*, 527–533.

Grinker, R. R. (1953). *Psychosomatic research.* New York: W. W. Norton.

Groen, J. J. et al. (1973). *Psychosomatische Aspecten van Diabetes Mellitus.* Amsterdam: De Erven Bohn.

Gross, J., & Svab, L. (1969). Die experimentelle sensorielle Deprivation als Modellsituation der psychotherapeutischen Beziehung. *Der Nervenarzt, 40*, 2.

Grossman, S. P. (1975). Role of the hypothalamus in the regulation of food and water intake. *Psychol Rev., 82*, 200. Cited in J. R. Brobeck (Ed.) (1979), *Best & Taylor's physiological basis of medical practice* (10th ed.). Baltimore: Williams & Wilkins.

Grunberger, B. (1971). *Le narcissisme.* Paris: Payot.

Habermas, T., & Müller, M. (1986). Das Bulimie-Syndrom: Krankheitsbild, Dynamik und Therapie. *Der Nervenarzt, 57*, 322–331.

Haenel, T., & Berger, W. (1984). *Group therapy with insulin dependant diabetic patients.* Ref. 27.3.1984, Congress: "Recent advances in psychiatric treatment," 1st European Conference, Vienna, March 25–30, 1984.

Halmi, K. (1980). Gastric bypass for massive obesity. In A. J. Stunkard (Ed.), *Obesity* (p. 388). Philadelphia, London, Toronto: W. B. Saunders.

Harju, E., & Fried, R. *Dysorexia as a family disorder. Three cases with an obese parent and an anorectic child.* Dept. of Physiology, Univ. of Oulu, Finland (unpublished manuscript).

Harlow, H. S. (1962). Cited in S. S.Tomkins, *Affects, imagery, consciousness, Vol. I.* New York: Springer.

Harlow, H. S., & Harlow, M. K. (1967). Reifungsfaktoren im sozialen Verhalten. *Psyche, 2*, 193.

Hartmann, H. (1964). *Essays on ego psychology—selected problems in psychoanalytic theory.* New York: Int. Univ. Press.

Helweg-Larsen P., Hoffmeyer, H., Kieler, J., Thaysen, J. G., Thygesen, P., & Wulff, M. H. (1952). Famine disease in German concentration camps, complications and sequels. *Acta Scand. Suppl., 274*, Vol. 44.

Henry, J. P., & Ely, D. L. (1976). Biologic correlates of psychosomatic illness. In R. G. Grenell & S. Gabay (Eds.), *Biological foundations of psychiatry, Vol. 2*, 1945–1985. New York: Raven. Cited in J. P. Henry & P. M. Stephens (Eds.), *Stress, health, and the social environment. A sociobiologic approach to medicine.* New York, Heidelberg, Berlin: Springer-Verlag.

Herzig, E. A. (1978). *Betreuung Sterbender.* Basel: Rocom, Edition Roche.

Hetherington, A. W., & Ranson, S. W. (1940). Hypothalamic lesions and adiposity in the rat. *Anat. Rec. 78*, 419. Cited in J. R. Brobeck (Ed.) (1979), *Best & Taylor's physiological basis of medical practice* (10th ed.). Baltimore: Williams & Wilkins.

Hinkle, L. E. et al. (1949). Experimental study of life situations, emotions and the occurrence of acidosis in a juvenile diabetic. *Am. J. M. St., 27*, 30.

Hinkle, L. E. et al. (1951). Studies in diabetes mellitus III. *Psychosm. Med., 3,* 60.

Hinkle, L. E. et al. (1951). Studies in diabetes mellitus IV. *Psychosom. Med., 3,* 84.

Hinkle, L. E. et al. (1952). Importance of life stress in course of a management of diabetes mellitus IV. *Psychosom. Med., 3,* 84.

Hirsch, J., & Han, P. W. (1969). Cellularity of rat adipose tissue: Effect of growth, starvation and obesity. *J. Lipid. Res., 10,* 77. Cited in J. R. Brobeck (Ed.) (1979), *Best & Taylor's physiological basis of medical practice* (10th ed.). Baltimore: Williams & Wilkins.

Hoebel, B. G., & Teitelbaum, P. (1966). Weight regulation in normal and hypothalamic hyperphagic rats. *J. Comp. Physiol. Psychol. 6,* 819. Cited in J. R. Brobeck (Ed.) (1979), *Best & Taylor's physiological basis of medical practice* (10th ed.). Baltimore: Williams & Wilkins.

Kafka, F. (1935). Ein Hungerkünstler. In F. Kafka, *Die Erzählungen* (p. 75). Berlin: Schocken; Zürich: Buchclub Ex Libris.

Kaplan, L. P. (1966). Some observations from conjoint individual and group therapy with obese women. *Int. J. Group Psychother., 6,* 357–366.

Katz, D. (1932). *Hunger und Appetit.* Leipzig: Barth. Cited in V. Pudel & J. E. Meyer (1981), Zur Pathogenese und Therapie der Adipositas. *Der Nervenarzt, 52,* 250–260.

Keel, P. (1988). *Bulimie: Krankheitsbild, Abgrenzung, Psychodynamik und Behandlung.* Manuscript.

Keller, S. (1981). *Diebstähle bei Depressiven.* Diss., Basel.

Keller, S., Battegay, R., Rauchfleisch, U., & Haenel, T. (1981). Diebstähle bei Depressiven. *Monatschr. f. Kriminologie und Strafrechtsreform, 64,* 342.

Kennedy, G. C. (1953). The role of depot fat in the hypothalamic control of food intake in the rat. *Proc. R. Soc. Lond. Ser. B, 40,* 578. Cited in J. R. Brobeck (Ed.) (1979), *Best & Taylor's physiological basis of medical practice* (10th ed.). Baltimore: Williams & Wilkins.

Kernberg, O. (1975). Zur Behandlung narzisstischer Persönlichkeitsstörungen. *Psyche, 219,* 81–90.

Kernberg, O. (1975). *Borderline conditions and pathological narcissism.* New York: Jason Aronson.

Kernberg, O. (1981). Borderline disorders: Structural interviewing. *Psychiatric Clinics of North America, 4,* 619.

Kernberg, O. (1984). *Severe personality diorders: Psychotherapeutic strategies.* New Haven, London: Yale University Press.

Kielholz, A. (1920). Symbolische Diebstähle. *Z. Neurol. Psychiatr., 55,* 303

Klein, M. (1932). *The psychoanalysis of children.* London: Hogarth.

Klein, M. (1935). A contribution to the psychogenesis of manic-depressive states. *Int. J. Psychoanal., 6.*

Klein, M. (1940). Mourning and its relation to manic-depressive states. *Int. J. Psychoanal., 2,* 125–153.

Klessmann, E., & Klessman, H. (1988). *Heiliges Fasten, heilloses Fasten.* Bern, Stuttgart, Toronto: Hans Huber.

Kohen, G. (1946). *Retour d'Auschwitz, Souvenirs du Déporté 7419419.* Coulommiers, Paris: Imprim. Brodard et Taupin.

Kohut, H. (1971). *The analysis of the self.* New York: Int. Univ. Press.

Kohut, H. (1977). *The restoration of the self.* New York: Int. Univ. Press.

Kübler-Ross, E. (1973). *Interviews mit Sterbenden.* Stuttgart: Kreuz.

Labhardt F. (1964). Körperliches und seelisches Krankheitsgeschehen bei Depressiven und Süchtigen als Ausdruck einer Persönlichkeitsstörung. *Praxis, 53,* 1083.

Langsdorff, M. (1986). *Die heimliche Sucht, unheimlich zu essen.* Frankfurt a.M.: Fischer.

Lassiter R. E., & Willet A. B. (1973). Interaction of group cotherapists in the multidisciplinary team treatment of obesity. *Int. J. Group Psychother., 23,* 82–92.

Lempp, R. (1967). *Extrembelastung im Kindes- und Jugendalter.* Bern, Stuttgart, Wien: Hans Huber.

Luban-Plozza, B., & Pöldinger, W. (1971). *Der psychosomatisch Kranke in der Praxis.* München: Hans Huber.

Mahler, M. S. (1968). *On human symbiosis and the vicissitudes of individuation, Vol. I: Infantile psychosis.* New York: Int. Univ. Press.

Mann, T. (1951). Enttäuschung. In *Der kleine Herr Friedemann und andere Novellen.* Berlin: Fischer.

Margules D. L., Moisset, B., Lewis, M. J., Shibuya, H., & Pert, C. B. (1978). Beta-endorphin is associated with overeating in genetically obese mice (ob/ob) and rats (fa/fa). *Science, 202,* 988–991.

Marx, K. (1872). *Das Kapital. Kritik der politischen Oekonomie.* Berlin: Kiepenheuer. *(2nd edition, 1932.)*

Masterson, J. L. (1976). *Psychotherapy of the borderline adult.* New York: Brunner & Mazel.

Mayer, J., Bates, M. W. (1952). Blood glucose and food intake in normal and hypophysectomized, alloxan-treated rats. *Am. J. Physiol., 68,* 82.

McCloy, J., McCloy, R. R. (1979). Enkephalins, hunger, and obesity. *Lancet, ii,* 56. Cited in A. Pradalier, J. C. Willer, F. Boureau, & J. Dry (1980). Pain and obesity. *Lancet,* May 7, 1090–1091.

Medbak, S., Wass, J. A. H., Clement-Jones, V., Cooke, E. D., Bowcock, S. A., Cudworth, A. G., & Rees, L. N. (1981). Chlorpropamide alcohol flush and circulating metenkephaline: A positive lince. *Brit. Med. J., 283,* 927.

Mende, W. (1967). Zur Kriminologie depressiver Verstimmungen. *Der Nervenarzt, 38,* 546.

Mester, H. (1981). *Die Anorexia nervosa.* Berlin, Heidelberg, New York: Springer-Verlag.

Miller, A. (1979). *Das Drama des begabten Kindes und die Suche nach dem wahren Selbst.* Frankfurt a.M.: Suhrkamp.

Mirsky, A. (1958). Physiologic, psychologic and social determinants in the etiology of duodenal ulcer. *Am. J. of Digestive Diseases, (New Series) 3,* 285.

Mirsky, A. (1961/1962). Körperliche und seelische und soziale Faktoren bei psychosomatischen Störungen. *Psyche, 15,* 26.

Mitchell, J. E., Hatuskami, D., Eckert, E. D., & Pyle, R. L. (1985). Characteristics of 275 patients with bulimia. *Am. J. Psychiatry, 42,* 482–485.

Morley, A. (1980). The neuroendocrine control of appetite: The role of the endogenous opiates, cholecystokinin, TRH, Gamma-amino-butyric-acid and the diazepam receptor. *Life Sciences, 27,* 355–368.

Morley, J. E. ., Levine, A. S. (1980). Stress-induced eating is mediated through endogenous opiates. *Science, 209,* 1259–1260.

Oesterheld, J. R., McKenna, M. S., & Gould, N. B. (1987). Group psychotherapy of bulimia: A critical review. *Int. J. Group Psychother., 37,* 163–184.

Paul, Th., Meyer, J. E., & Pudel, V. (1987). Bulimia nervosa—Das Krankheitsbild und die Frage seiner nosologischen Zuordnung. *Der Nervenarzt, 58,* 461–470.

Perini, Ch., Rauchfleisch, U., & Bühler, F. R. (1982). *Personality structure and renine-type in essential hypertension.*

Perls, F. S. (1969). *Ego, hunger and aggression.* London: Allen & Unwin Ltd., 1947; New York: Random House, Vintage Books

Portmann, A. (1944). *Vom Ursprung des Menschen.* Basel: Reinhardt.

Pradalier, A., Willer, J. C., Boureau, F., & Dry, J. (1980). Pain and obesity. *Lancet, May 7,* 1090–1091.

Pudel, V., & Meyer, J.-E. (1981). Zur Pathogenese und Therapie der Adipositas. *Der Nervenarzt, 52,* 250–260.

Rank, O. (1924). *Das Trauma der Geburt und seine Bedeutung für die Psychoanalyse.* Leipzig, Wien, Zürich: Internationaler Psychoanalytischer Verlag

Rauchfleisch, U. (1979). *Handbuch zum Rosenzweig Picture-Frustration Test (PTF), Vol. I and II.* Bern, Stuttgart, Wien: Hans Huber.

Rauchfleisch, U. (1981). *Dissozial. Entwicklung, Struktur und Psychodynamik dissozialer Persönlichkeiten.* Göttingen: Vandenhoeck & Ruprecht

Rentchnik, P., Haynal, A., & de Senarclens, P. (1977). *Les orphelins, mènent— ils le monde?* Paris: Stock.

Robertson, J., & Robertson, J. (1972). Quality of substitute care as an influence on separation responses. *J. of Psychosomatic Research, 16,* 261.

Robertson, J., & Robertson, J. (1975). Reaktionen kleiner Kinder auf kurzfristige Trennungen von der Mutter im Lichte neuer Beobachtungen. *Psyche, 29,* 626.

Rohde-Dachser, Ch. (1982). *Das Borderline-Syndrom.* Bern, Stuttgart, Wien: Hans Huber. (2nd edition, 1979).

Rosenman, R. H. (1971). The central nervous system and coronary heart disease. *Hosp. Pract., 6,* 87–97.

Rosenman, R. H., Brand, R. J., Jenkins, C. D., Friedman, M., Straus, R., & Wurm, M. (1975). Coronary heart disease in the Western Collaborative Group Study. Final follow-up experience of 8½ years. *J. Am. Med. Assoc., 233,* 872–877. Cited in J. P. Henry & P. M. Stephens (Eds.) (1977), *Stress, health, and the social environment. A sociobiologic approach to medicine.* New York, Heidelberg, Berlin: Springer-Verlag.

Rosenman, R. H., Brand, R. J., Sholtz, R. I., & Friedman, M. (1976). Multivariate prediction of coronary heart disease during 8½ year follow-up in the

Western Collaborative Group Study. *Am. J. Cardiol.*, *37*, 903–910. Cited in J. P. Henry & P. M. Stephens (Eds.) (1977), *Stress, health, and the social environment. A sociobiologic approach to medicine.* New York, Heidelberg, Berlin: Springer-Verlag.

Rotter, J. I., Sones, J. Q., Samloff, I. M., Richardson, Ch. T., Gursky, J. M., Walsh, J. H., & Rimond, D. L. (1979). Duodenal-ulcer disease associated with elevated serum pepsinogen I. *New England J. of Med.*, *300*, 63.

Russek, M. (1975). Current hypotheses in the control of feeding behaviour. In G. J. Mogenson & F. R. Calaresu (Eds.), *Neural integration of physiological mechanisms and behaviour* (p. 28). Toronto: Univ. Toronto Press. Cited in J. R. Brobeck (Ed.) (1979), *Best & Taylor's physiological basis of medical practice* (10th ed.). Baltimore: Williams & Wilkins

Saudek, C. D., & Felig, Ph. (1976), The metabolic events of starvation. *Am. J. Med.*, *60*, 117.

Schachter, S., & Singer, J. E. (1962). Cognitive, social and physiological determinants of emotional state. *Psychol. Rev.*, *619*, 379–399.

Schindler, W.. (1968). Personal communication.

Schütze, G. (1980). *Anorexia nervosa.* Bern, Stuttgart, Wien: Hans Huber.

Schwarz, J. (1962). *Mein Kampf auf Leben und Tod, Leidensweg eines KZ-Häftlings.* Köln: Bachem.

Sifneos, P. E. (1973). The prevalence of "alexithymic" characteristics in psychosomatic patients. *Psychotherapy and Psychosomatics*, *22*, 255.

Smith, G. P. (1976). Humoral hypotheses for the control of food intake. In G. A. Bray (Ed.), *Obesity in perspective* (Vol. 2, pt. 2, p. 19). U.S. Govt Printing Office. Cited in J. R. Brobeck (Ed.) (1979), *Best & Taylor's physiological basis of medical practice* (10th ed.). Baltimore: Williams & Wilkins.

Sours, J. A. (1980). *Starving to death in a sea of objects: The Anorexia nervosa syndrome.* New York: Jason Aronson.

Spitz, R. A. (1957/1960). *Die Entstehung der ersten Objektbeziehungen.* Stuttgart: Klett.

Spitz, R. A. (1965). *The first year of life.* New York: Int. Univ. Press.

Statistical Bulletin Metrop. Life Insur. Co. (1959) Nr. 40, Nov./Dec. Cited in *Wiss. Tab. Geigy* (p. 70). Basel: Geigy.

Stauder, K. H. (1959). Studien zur Psychologie und Psychotherapie der Fettsüchtigen. *Psyche*, *2*, 641–686.

Stern, D., & Beebe, B. (1977). Engagement-disengagement and early object experiences. In N. Freedman & S. Grand (Eds.), *Communicative structures and psychic structures.* New York: Plenum.

Stevens, E., & Salisbury, J. (1984). A cognitive behavioral group treatment of bulimia. *Brit. J. Psychiatry*, *46*, 66–69. Cited in J. R. Oesterheld, M. S. McKenna, & N. B. Gould (1987), Group psychotherapy of bulimia: A critical review. *Int. J. Group Psychother.*, *37*.

Stierlin, G., & Bruch, H. (1980). *Der goldene Käfig/Das Rätsel der Magersucht.* Frankfurt a.M.: S. Fischer.

Stunkard, A. J. (1980). Psychoanalysis and psychotherapy. In A. J. Stunkard (Ed.), *Obesity* (p. 355). Philadelphia, London, Toronto: W. B. Saunders.

Stunkard, A. J., & Fox, S. (1971). The relationship of gastric motility and hunger. *Psychosom. Med., 33,* 123–134.

Stunkard, A. J., Grace, W. J., & Wolff, H. (1959). The nighteating syndrome. *American J. Medicine, 19,* 78.

Teitelbaum, P., & Stellar, E. (1954). Recovery from the failure to eat produced by hypothalamic lesions. *Science, 20,* 894. Cited in J. R. Brobeck (Ed.) (1979), *Best & Taylor's physiological basis of medical practice* (10th ed.). Baltimore: Williamson & Wilkins.

Thomae, H. (1961). *Anorexia nervosa.* Bern: Hans Huber, Stuttgart: Klett.

Von Baeyer, W., & Kisker, K. P. (1960). Abbiegung der Persönlichkeitsentwicklung eines Jugendlichen durch nationalsozialistische Verfolgungen. Paranoide Fehlhaltung. In H. March (Ed.), *Verfolgung und Angst* (p. 11). Stuttgart: Klett.

Wallace, M., Fraser, Ch., Clements, J. A., & Funder, J. W. (1981). Naloxone, adrenalectomy, and steroid replacement: Evidence against a role for circulating beta-endorphin in food intake. *Endocrinol, 108,* 189–192.

Wilkinson, D. G. (1981). Psychiatric aspects of diabetes mellitus. *Brit. J. Psychiat., 38,* 1.

Willi, J. (1975). *Die Zweierbeziehung.* Reinbek: Rowohlt.

Winnicott, D. W. (1971). *Playing and reality.* London: Tavistock Publications.

Zorn, F. (1977). *Mars.* Munich: Kindler.

❖Author Index

148

❖Subject Index

E

Early
–childhood 6-8, 10, 16, 17, 21, 25, 38, 41, 47, 51, 53, 54, 57, 59, 61, 69, 71, 74, 80, 90, 103, 107, 123, 129-131
–deficiency 6
–psychoanalysis 37

Eating
–attacks 86
–behavior 13, 14, 20, 21-27, 29-34, 38, 39, 47-49, 66, 84-87, 111, 113
–habits 48
–orgy 21
–pattern 14

EEG 8

Ego 11, 25, 27, 54, 60, 65, 66, 69, 70, 75, 77-81, 106, 124, 125, 131
–cores 54
–fragmentation 25, 54, 69, 75, 79, 80, 124, 131
–functions 27, 124
–ideal 125
–strength 106
–weakness 54, 77, 78, 131

Eliminating the object 77

Emotional
–attention 9, 47, 69, 89, 93
–deficiency 14, 22, 47
–deprivation 9
–hunger 4, 6, 9, 10, 14, 22, 83, 90, 92, 105-110
–nourishment 36, 47, 83, 89, 90, 102
–relationship 9, 10, 37
–satisfaction 11
–trauma 84
–warmth 11, 37, 69, 85, 90

Empathy/empathic interest 11, 19

Encephaline 87

Endogenous
–endorphine 29
–(major) depressions 60, 131
–morphine 29
–opiates 29, 87

Endorphine/endorphine system 29, 87

Energetic reserves (fats) 111

Epilepsy 72, 73

Escape strategy 16

Essential hypertension 38, 43, 97, 98, 135

Esthetics 22

Evaluation 45, 74, 89

Expectation 6, 25, 37, 38, 47, 51, 53, 61, 69, 71, 77, 92, 100, 103, 120, 126, 131, 134

Expression 11

Expressive, psychoanalytically oriented psychotherapy 80

Extended suicide 79

External stimuli 34

Extinguishing the object 77

Eye language 11

F

Face mask 10

Familial disposition 26, 56

Family 7, 15, 18, 20, 22, 23, 25, 26, 35, 36, 56, 71, 72, 74, 78, 91, 99, 107-110
–history 25, 26, 78

Fantasy
–of granduer 69, 70
–of grandiosity 118, 123, 125

Fasting 111-113

Fasting regimen 112

Feelings
–of guilt 35, 86, 89, 109, 126
–of inferiority 7

Females 14-17, 21, 25, 27, 36, 40, 48, 78

Female
–adolescents 14, 17, 21
–adult role 14

Final solution 125

Follow-up study 42, 47, 92

Food
–control behavior 13
–deprivation 111
–intake/-behavior 13, 14, 20-24, 26, 27, 29-34, 38, 39, 47-49, 66, 84-87, 111, 113
    – center 13, 29, 85
    – practice 48
    – rituals 48
–refusal 14, 87

Fragmentation of ego 25, 54, 69, 75, 79, 80, 124, 131

Freedom 1, 17, 77-79, 117, 118, 130

Frustration 6, 21, 26, 37, 38, 61, 63, 72, 75, 90, 94

Fur mother 9, 10

Fuse/fusion 1, 24-26, 34, 36-38, 47, 48, 51-57, 61, 65, 66, 69-81, 92, 94, 102, 124-126, 129
– with an idealized self-object 53

G

Gastric ulcer 64, 65, 93, 94, 135

Gastrointestinal
–cancer 90
–disturbances 4, 58, 89-95, 134, 135

Genetic
–disposition 56, 74, 123
–factors 83, 131, 135
–predisposition 69, 71, 80, 86

Gestalt-cognition 8, 10, 54, 71

National Socialism (Nazi) 7, 11, 112-114, 124-126, 136
Natural
–feeding 5, 89, 90
–order 70
Nearness 5, 6, 36, 51
Necrophilia 70, 71
Necrophilic character 70
Neurotic infantilism 41
Newborn 5, 6, 8, 129
Nitrogen elimination 111, 112
Noncompliance 85
Norepinephrine 29, 30, 98
Nourishment 5, 6, 8-10, 13, 19, 22, 36-38, 47, 83, 89, 90, 102, 115, 129
Nurses 107, 108

O

Obesity/obese persons 12-14, 22, 27, 29-49, 67, 85, 111, 112, 130
Object 9, 19, 22-26, 33, 34, 36-38, 47, 48, 51-57, 60, 61, 63, 65, 66, 69-81, 85, 86, 92, 94, 111, 123-127, 129, 130, 132, 135
–deprivation 85
–representation 34, 37, 69, 73, 75, 77-80, 123, 129, 130
–value 129
Obsession 21
Oedipal neurosis 41
Ontogenetic development 13
Opiate/opiate antagonist 29, 87
Oral
–antidiabetic drug 87
–hunger 88
–incorporation 86, 94
–incorporative relationship 36, 65
–need 11

–satisfaction 89, 93
Orality 5, 6, 37, 89, 93
Organic brain disorder 73, 117
Orphanage 72, 89
Overactivity 97-103
Overprotection 25, 61, 69, 103, 120, 129
Overweight 24, 46

P

Pancreas 87, 112
Pantomimic expression 11
Paranoid
–disorder 74, 75
–ideas 75
Parliamentary control 124, 125
Pattern of solving problems 26, 28, 36
Penal Code 73
Pepsinogen/-concentration 92-94, 111, 134
Peristatic inducibility 39
Personality disorder 26, 27, 75
Physical nourishment 115
Physician 105-110, 136
Politics/politician 6, 7, 53, 99, 123-127, 132, 133
Political power 126
Population classes 118
Possession 9, 19, 22-26, 33-38, 47, 53, 57, 60, 63, 65, 66, 71, 79, 85, 86, 111, 123, 124, 129, 130, 132, 135
Power 6, 7, 75, 83, 98, 115, 123, 124, 126, 127, 132, 133
Power reasons 133
Predisposition 69, 71, 80, 86
Prevalence 16
Primates 5, 37, 129

Problem-solving behavior 16
Professional life 119, 120
Prognosis 16, 18, 26, 81, 105-107
Projective identification 70, 79, 80, 124, 125
Proletariats 133
Protection 47, 90
Protein catabolism 111-113
Psychiatric diagnoses 40
Psychic humiliation 113
Psychoanalysis/psychoanalyst 6, 36, 38, 48, 52, 80, 85
Psychoanalytic
–cognitive basis
–treatment 48
Psychoanalytically oriented therapy 85
Psychosomatic
–disorders 11, 92
–process 12
Psychotherapy/-therapist 15-20, 24, 26, 27, 36, 39, 42, 43, 46-49, 52, 63, 73, 80, 84, 92, 100, 102, 107, 108, 136
Psychotherapy
–group 39
–program 20
Puberty 17, 18, 21, 41

R

Rage 7, 70, 75, 125
Rats/rat trials 13, 14, 29, 30, 31
Reality 47, 55, 56, 58, 61, 64, 69, 71, 73, 76, 94, 99, 107, 126, 127, 131, 133
Real self 51, 53, 103
Recognition 24, 26, 52, 62, 75, 80, 81, 83, 86, 92, 99, 113, 123, 129, 131, 133
Refusal of food 24

WM175 ~~KILLER~~ BAT